THE COLLECTED WORKS OF JUPITER HAMMON

THE COLLECTED WORKS OF
Jupiter Hammon

———

Poems and Essays

———

EDITED AND WITH
AN INTRODUCTION BY
Cedrick May

The University of Tennessee Press | Knoxville

Library of Congress Cataloging-in-Publication Data
Names: Hammon, Jupiter, 1711– approximately 1800, author.
| May, Cedrick, 1969- editor.
Title: The collected works of Jupiter Hammon : poems and essays /
edited and   with an introduction by Cedrick May.
Description: First edition. | Knoxville : The University of Tennessee Press,
[2017] | Includes bibliographical references.
Identifiers: LCCN 2016053323| ISBN 9781621903291
(hardcover : alk. paper) |
ISBN 9781621903314
Classification: LCC PS767 .H15 2017 | DDC 811/.1--dc23
LC record available at https://lccn.loc.gov/2016053323

To my mom,
Letta M. May

Contents

Foreword

It is always a delight to learn about the discovery of new texts by poets, especially those created by Early American poets, and even more particularly to see new texts by African-American poets. As I am presently compiling an anthology of eighteenth-century American poetry, I certainly enjoy the opportunity to add to the selections by Jupiter Hammon.

"An Essay on Slavery" and "Dear Hutchinson is Dead and Gone" constitute substantial additions to Hammon's oeuvre. The poet's anti-slavery piece ably articulates Hammon's conviction that all slaves must be free. And his elegy on Miss Hutchinson includes a traceable awareness of the structure of the typical Puritan funeral elegy of the time. Opening with a description of Hutchinson's worthy life (her "chosen" disposition, her walking in the way of God's wisdom, her exemplary behavior shown to others, and her frequent practice of faithful prayer), moving to her flight to God (an apotheosis of sorts), followed by the poet's urging her parents not to grieve, then his description of a procession of mourners, and finally his closing exhortation to the living to follow the deceased's example all depict the typical Puritan elegy. Actually this poem accords well with the kind of elegy Phillis Wheatley composed.

What these newly recovered poems by Hammon tell us is that he was a much more complex poet than we have guessed. Cedrick May has now enabled us to recognize a much clearer knowledge of Hammon's achievement. As well, May reveals a generosity toward the work of earlier scholars of Hammon. For example, he praises the work of such excellent scholars as Phillip M. Richards, Sondra A. O'Neale, Lonnell E. Johnson, Margaret A. Brucia, and Arlen Nydam.

Ordinarily one expects to find notes to edited texts to be "dry as dust." Such is hardly the case here. Indeed, I find May's 251 notes to be fascinating, learned, and a joy to read. For example, one discovers informative tracts on astronomy, Milton, and especially on biblical passages. On p. 13, for example, one encounters keys to one of many puzzles which pepper Hammon's numerous references to the biblical text. Note 1 informs us Hammon, as on several occasions, is intensely concerned to pursue the importance of spiritual (as opposed to material) wealth.

Note 29, beginning on p. 35 and ending on p. 36, is actually a brief but pithy essay which explores further Hammon's penchant to seek his spiritual freedom. Just a few notes beyond this one (note 36), we see how May describes the sacking and occupation of Hartford by the British during the Revolutionary War.

Seldom have I come across so artfully prepared an edition as Cedrick May's *Collected Works of Jupiter Hammon*. It will surely be a pleasure to read and a joy to use in the classroom.

John C. Shields
Illinois State University

Preface

The volume you hold before you gathers all of the known written works of the eighteenth-century American poet and slave named Jupiter Hammon. It represents not only the known works of Jupiter Hammon, but also a major effort to reevaluate his literary canon within a significantly expanded body of literary and biographical information discovered about the author between October 2011 and the summer of 2015. This new edition of Jupiter Hammon's known works introduces readers to newly discovered writings by the author, while adding information and insights into Hammon's life story that complicates many traditional readings of Hammon as a "complacent" slave. This new edition constitutes a radical re-reading of Hammon as a much more complex and intellectually curious commentator on his historical and political period.

Jupiter Hammon was born into slavery on October 17, 1711, in a newly built saltbox manor house on Long Island. Jupiter's parents were Rose and Obium, a couple whose own parents were enslaved and brought to the Americas in the late seventeenth century.[1] Hammon was born in a house owned by Henry Lloyd, a wealthy and influential New England merchant, and like the rest of the property on the Lloyd plantation, he owned Jupiter, just as he owned the child's parents.

Jupiter grew up on the isolated island community of the Long Island plantation among the other enslaved servants and the Lloyd family. Hammon's story is unique in that he grew up alongside and with several of Henry Lloyd's own children who were around the same age and learned to read and write. Because of this early education, Hammon developed a level of literacy unusual for slaves and servants during the early eighteenth century. During his lifetime, Hammon was a notable member within the community of slaves on Long Island and in Hartford and New Haven, Connecticut, places he was forced to flee to for safety during the American Revolutionary War. In the second half of his long life, he published several poems and essays, and it is speculated that he may have been a lay preacher among the other enslaved community members. These writings form the basis for this book, this new edition of Jupiter Hammon's known works.

Although Hammon was born in 1711, it appears he did not begin publishing his writings until 1760 with his first known poem, "An Evening Thought," when he was forty-nine years old. Hammon seems to have ended his career as a writer upon the delivery and publication of his most (in)famous piece of writing, "An Address to the Negroes in the State of New-York," to the members of the African Society of New York City on September 24, 1786. Although the "Address" was thought by scholars to be Hammon's final work, a previously unknown, handwritten poem was discovered in the archives of Yale University's Sterling Library in October 2011.[2] The discovery of the new poem and the body of original research I have analyzed over the last decade convinced me that a new edition of Jupiter Hammon's works was needed for the current generation of twenty-first-century students, teachers, and researchers of early African-American literature.

The work of editing an edition of any Early American writer's work requires a tremendous amount of labor and careful attention to detail. Previous editors of Hammon's writings have produced important editions that well served the needs of their time. It is my belief that the widespread knowledge of the very existence of Jupiter Hammon's works during the twentieth century is owed to Oscar Wegelin and Stanley A. Ransom, Jr.

Wegelin was an enthusiastic collector and bibliophile who published a slim collection of four of Hammon's known poems in 1915, after he discovered the existence of one of Hammon's lost poems, "An Evening Thought," in the collections of the New-York Historical Society.[3] Wegelin's book reintroduced Hammon's writings to a reading public that had long forgotten the enslaved poet. A very important part of the book was an annotated bibliography that listed the locations of Hammon's known works.[4]

Although Oscar Wegelin reintroduced Hammon to readers in 1915, it was the work of Stanley A. Ransom that kept Hammon's works in the public eye and in schools through the second half of the twentieth century. His 1970 edition, *America's First Negro Poet: The Complete Works of Jupiter Hammon of Long Island*, assembled for the first time all of Hammon's known poetry and prose. This compilation of Hammon's works was tremendously important for illustrating the writer's range as both a poet and an essayist. The edition also included reprints of two essays about Jupiter Hammon, a biographical sketch by Oscar Wegelin, and a critical analysis of Hammon's works by Vernon Loggins, as well as reprinting Wegelin's annotated bibliography.[5]

It is also important to note Sondra A. O'Neale's book, *Jupiter Hammon and the Biblical Beginnings of African-American Literature* (Scarecrow Press 1993). Though O'Neale's book is a critical monograph of Hammon's work, and not an edition, the book is one of the first instances of contemporary scholarship that attempts to fairly evaluate Hammon's work within the context of American slavery. O'Neale's analysis of Hammon's biblical allusions and her overriding argument that Hammon's poetry and prose were an act of subversive resistance against chattel slavery break the traditional mold of Hammon scholarship and are foundational for the reemergence of modern Hammon studies.

Each of these works by Wegelin, Ransom, and O'Neale represents a direct line of descent, a line that performed the hard work of keeping Jupiter Hammon's poetry and prose publicly available through scholarship and useful editions of the poet's works. Many literary anthologies owe a debt of gratitude to the work already done by these previous editors, each of them updating and revising our perception and reception of Jupiter Hammon, the poet and enslaved American. I also owed a debt of gratitude to Wegelin, Ransom, and O'Neale for making Hammon's works available to me, even if only as reprints that had to be purchased in used book stores. This was especially the case with Wegelin and Ransom—their editions of Jupiter Hammon's poetry and prose have been out of print for several decades—and O'Neale's monograph has also seen the end of its publication run and is no longer easy to find, which brings us to the importance of the present edition.

Jupiter Hammon is a poet and essayist whose works have been established as a foundation for contemporary African-American literary studies. Although his works are well recognized for their importance to the canon, and some of his poems regularly appear in anthologies of American and African-American literature, there has not been a carefully edited edition of his works available for decades. This edition is the answer to that longstanding problem. Not only does this edition, *The Collected Works of Jupiter Hammon*, reintroduce Hammon's works to the public, it adds to the canon of Jupiter Hammon's known works with two newly discovered poems and integrates a decade of research into Hammon's life and writings that adds significantly to what we know about Jupiter Hammon's life story, as well as his literature. While I stand on the shoulders of the great editors, scholars, and writers who came before me, this edition will further contribute to the study of Jupiter Hammon at all levels in a number of ways, both large and subtle.

One of the most important differences between this edition of Hammon's works and all previous ones is my effort to maintain, as closely as possible, the *presentation* of the individual works as they first appeared in print. For instance, all of the previous editors of Hammon's works divided his poetry and prose into separate sections within their editions, giving the impression that Hammon wrote and published all of his poetry and prose as completely independent works at different times, when in fact two of his poems were published as *conclusions* to the essays they accompanied. Placing these essays and poems in context with one another significantly changes the ways contemporary readers will understand and interpret their contents. This is especially true for the ways readers approach Hammon's third and final known essay, which was published twice in 1787, but is the only one of Hammon's three essays that was printed without a concluding poem.

Another major difference between this edition of Jupiter Hammon's works and earlier ones is that I include information about one of Hammon's lost works, "An Essay on the Ten Virgins." I do this within the context of his other known works. Although we have not yet found a copy of this lost poem, I think it is diligent to acknowledge it as a significant part of Hammon's publishing history, especially given the recent discovery of two previously unknown poems, "Dear Hutchinson is Dead and Gone" and "An Essay on Slavery." I also make an effort to speculate on what this poem that is currently lost to us might have looked like, based on research about Hammon's reading and habits of writing, as well as what can be known about his theological training based on books at his disposal and ideas he drew from scholarly theological sources. Vernon Loggins concludes in his essay included in the Ransom edition of Hammon's works that, "Whatever advantages and privileges the Lloyds might have granted him, there is no indication in his writings that they gave him opportunity for instruction beyond the most elementary training in reading and writing."[6] This is a peculiar assertion that should be categorically rejected by readers of Jupiter Hammon's works, and I will explain how we can construct an accurate catalog of Hammon's literary and theological sources and reading materials through a close reading of his works, as well as with documentary evidence of the books available to him in the households of his masters, the Lloyd family.

Finally, and most important for Hammon scholarship of the last half-century and the beginning of this current one, is the discovery of previously lost, unknown, and unpublished poems that were discovered in holograph form, "Dear Hutchinson is Dead and Gone" and "An Essay on Slavery." "An Essay on Slavery," itself, is a remarkable contribution to Hammon scholarship and African-American literary history in its own right, but as I shall argue, it also allows us deeper insight into Jupiter Hammon's personal feelings about the institution of slavery. I place "An Essay on Slavery" as the concluding poem of Hammon's most famous work, "An Address to the Negroes in the State of New-York," because

I believe Hammon intended it to be published along with the essay as a single document—the same way that "A Poem for Children With Thoughts on Death" [*sic*] and "A Dialogue, Intitled, The Kind Master and Dutiful Servant" [*sic*] were published as conclusions of longer works, thus revealing a formal literary continuity in Hammon's writing style. Placing "An Essay on Slavery" alongside "An Address to the Negroes in the State of New-York" will necessarily overturn previous readings of Hammon's most (in)famous essay and force us to reevaluate well over two-hundred years of its interpretation. Further, his most recently discovered poem, "Dear Hutchinson is Dead and Gone," a holograph draft discovered at the New-York Historical Society Library by Claire Bellerjeau, illustrates Hammon's depth and range of subjects, as well as a seeming interest in radical women protesters of the American religious and political status quo.

I first encountered Jupiter Hammon's writings as a graduate student and was struck instantly by the depth of his skill as a writer and with his ability to weave complex theological ideas into what *appeared* to be the poetry and prose of a burgeoning folk tradition. I then began to realize that Jupiter Hammon's writings were actually an early example of clear-eyed black intellectualism that addressed numerous historic, political, and spiritual problems of the writer's time period. When I began doing focused research on Hammon, I found at the time—in the late 1990s—that there was very little actual scholarship about him or his poetry and prose. In fact, Oscar Wegelin's 1915 biographical sketch appeared to be the primary source for every subsequent scholar's knowledge of Jupiter Hammon's biography. Since the publication of Wegelin's book, there were only a few notable pieces of original research that attempted to shed light on Hammon's life, including Charles A. Verantes's essay, "Jupiter Hammon: Early Negro Poet of Long Island" in *The Nassau County Historical Journal* (1957) and Phillip M. Richard's "Nationalist Themes in the Preaching of Jupiter Hammon" in *Early American Literature* (1990). The most important *archival* discovery in the twentieth century, after Wegelin's, was the discovery of Hammon's exact date of birth—October 17, 1711—by Louis Lomax, a professor of Humanities and Social Sciences at Hofstra University, and his graduate student, Lillian Koppel, early in 1970. That discovery was the last time Jupiter Hammon's biography had been updated in the scholarly record. It seemed obvious to me—after reading the same brief biographical sketches over and again—that there was much more to be discovered about this important literary and historic figure, and it was that incredible lack of original archival research and analysis that led me to pursue further knowledge about this eighteenth-century poet and American slave.

The Collected Works of Jupiter Hammon is meant to be an edition of his poetry and prose that will be of use to students and researchers alike. My intent is to be as conservative as possible about making changes to the text of Hammon's works while also making his poetry and prose as accessible as possible for modern readers. Emendations are made only in those cases where clarity is compromised. However, since this is an expanded edition of Hammon's known works, it is important for me to explain all of my "minor" changes, in addition to the major ones concerning *presentation* and *content* mentioned above. The following are editing choices I made globally to Hammon's collected works:

One of the most important editorial choices I make is to maintain the spelling of most words throughout his writings. I identify any spellings I change with footnotes.

The long S forms have been modernized for readability.

Ligatures such as ſt have also been modernized.

I consistently eliminate the extra space between the last word of a line and a semicolon terminating the line. This was a formatting quirk of the eighteenth century due to the way the lead semicolon type fit into the press adjacent to other characters.

I eliminate all end-of-line hyphens that break a word between two lines.

I have also eliminated the catchwords that appear throughout Hammon's printed essays and two of his poems.

Hammon quotes the King James Version of the Bible throughout his essays, but many of the quotations are misattributed. That is to say, the quotes that appear in Hammon's writing do not match the chapter and verse attributed to them in many instances. For instance, in "A Winter Piece," Hammon writes, "Let us contemplate on the manner of Christ's resurrection. Matt. xxv. 2. 'Behold there was a great earthquake, for the angel of the Lord descended from heaven, and came and rolled the stone from the door and sat upon it.'" Hammon attributes the biblical quote to the Book of Matthew 25:2. However, this is incorrect; the quoted passage is actually from Matthew 28:2. It is uncertain whether this is due to printers' errors or Hammon's own mistakes, but I have chosen to keep the references as originally printed and identify the mistaken ones for readers with notes.

There are many other emendations made to Hammon's original texts specific to each poem and essay. I have identified those emendations in the introduction to each literary work and with footnotes whenever they occur.

Each of Hammon's writings are formatted as closely as possible to the original, but the two broadside poems collected here presented a particular challenge for presentation in contemporary book form. So, at the bottom of the first page of "An Evening Thought" and "An Address to Miss Phillis Wheatley" are instructions for reading the columns in their proper order, a compromise that allows readers to see the poems close to their original form.

All of Hammon's works appearing in this volume are original transcriptions of his published works and unpublished holograph drafts collected from the various libraries and archives where the originals are located. In most cases, these copy-texts were reproduced through high-definition scanning so I would have a reliable reproduction in my possession after finishing my work in the archives, and thus be able to proof my transcriptions as I completed the edition.

NOTES

1. For a detailed account of Jupiter Hammon's family spanning seven generations beginning in West Africa, see Charla E. Bolton and Reginald H. Metcalf, Jr.'s groundbreaking 2013 essay about the Hammon family, "The Migration of Jupiter Hammon and His Family: From Slavery to Freedom and its Consequences," in the *Long Island History Journal*, lihj.cc.stonybrook.edu/2013/articles/the -migration-of-jupiter-hammon-and-his-family-from-slavery-to-freedom-and-its-consequences/.

2. For more information about the discovery of the unpublished poem, see my article, co-written with Julie McCown, "An Essay on Slavery: An Unpublished Poem by Jupiter Hammon." *Early American Literature,* vol. 48, no. 2, 2013, 457–71.

3. The full title of the poem is, "An Evening Thought. Salvation by Christ, With Penitential Cries" [*sic*]. The poem was published as a broadside dated December 25, 1760.

4. Wegelin, Oscar. *Jupiter Hammon: American Negro Poet, Selections from his Writings.* 1915. Reprint. Mnemosyne Publishing Co., Inc., 1969.

5. The Vernon Loggins critical essay in Ransom's edition was a conventional essay for its time. In it, Loggins compares Hammon's poetry to that of the more highly educated European poets popular during Hammon's lifetime; however, Loggins does reveal several interesting and original insights into Hammon's writing as "folk poetry," though he is adamant in his evaluation of the works as "artlessness." He also makes what I strongly believe are mistaken assumptions about Hammon's educational background and the nature of his religious upbringing. I would direct readers to Loggins's essay and then compare his thoughts to my own evaluation of Hammon's education and religious upbringing in the first chapter of my book, *Evangelism and Resistance in the Black Atlantic, 1760–1835.* U of Georgia P, 2008.

6. Ransom 36.

Acknowledgments

This volume is the result of over a decade of hard work, encouragement, support, and faith from many quarters.

I am grateful to Scot Danforth, director of the University of Tennessee Press, for his interest and unwavering support for this volume. Working with Scot and the press has been an unqualified pleasure. I would like to thank the copyeditor, Linda Parsons Marion, for the incredible work she performed on this very complicated text. I would also like to thank the reviewers of this book, whose comments and feedback helped to improve the volume. I am tremendously grateful for the enthusiasm shown by my readers, Scot, and the press's editorial board for this new edition.

I would also like to thank John C. Shields, who encouraged me at every stage of the project and was a marvelous sounding board for ideas and questions related to process. I am honored by his contribution of the foreword to this book and his friendship.

Carla J. Mulford introduced me to Jupiter Hammon when I was a graduate student in her Early American Literature course at Penn State University, drawing me into the field and introducing me to the mysteries of Hammon's life and poetry. I cannot thank Carla enough for taking me on as a student and helping me to develop the discipline and skill to be a contributing professional in a field that continues to have so much to offer to the record of our shared cultural heritage.

I would like to thank Beth Wright, former dean of the College of Liberal Arts, and Ron Elsenbaumer, provost at the University of Texas at Arlington, who each contributed to funding research trips that resulted in the discovery of many of the documents mentioned in this book. These documents, uncovered with their support and that of the university, help shed light on long-forgotten aspects of Jupiter Hammon's life and times. I owe a tremendous debt of gratitude to Bridget Lewis, assistant director for Media Relations at UT Arlington, who worked to make the discovery of a previously unknown poem by Jupiter Hammon—which appears in this volume—part of the national conversation through various news outlets, including a National Public Radio interview with

Michel Martin on her *Tell Me More* radio show. The tremendous reaction to the discovery of a poem by an early American of African descent reveals the perennial importance of liberal arts and humanities research to the public interest.

I would like to thank Yale University, the Beinecke Rare Books and Manuscript Library, and the Sterling Memorial Library for access to invaluable research materials that helped make this book possible. I would also like to thank Michael Warner, former Department of English chair at Yale University, who invited me to Yale to deliver a lecture on Jupiter Hammon. I benefited greatly from conversations with him and from the feedback I received on that occasion. Other organizations that deserve recognition include the Library of Congress, the New-York Historical Society, and the Connecticut Historical Society, all of which provided access to their holdings related to Jupiter Hammon.

I cannot overemphasize how grateful I am to the Society for the Preservation of Long Island Antiquities (SPLIA) for hosting me for a talk that resulted in enthusiastic feedback and helped me to think through some research questions in ways that I had not considered. SPLIA also gave me two days of access to both of the homes Jupiter Hammon spent most of his life inhabiting. Spending time in those spaces where Hammon was born, played as a child, and served as an adult helped me to conceptualize an internal life of the mind, as well as an external life of enslavement, that would have been his. I encourage everyone to support SPLIA's efforts to restore and preserve all of Long Island's historic buildings and artifacts, and the homes of Jupiter Hammon in particular.

I would also like to thank my father-in-law, Dr. Gerard J. Ingram, MD, whose medical expertise and research into Jupiter Hammon's life-threatening struggle with gout at the age of nineteen helped me to consider the long-term implications of that health crisis to Hammon's life history.

I owe a special debt of gratitude to Charla E. Bolton and the late Reginald H. Metcalf, Jr., both of whom worked together over many years to piece together Jupiter Hammon's family tree. Their tireless work and dedication to searching the archives has contributed greatly to what is and can be known about Jupiter Hammon.

I owe my greatest debt to my family. To Letta M. May, my mother, who encouraged me to soldier on through school on the many occasions when I was hungry and broke and close to the end of my endurance. Her example of lifelong strength and perseverance has always been a model for me. To Penny, my wife, who is my strength and eternal love, and without whom nothing I do would be possible. And to William and Thomas, my sons and my greatest joy in life.

Introduction

On the night of a bright, waxing half-moon, October 17, 1711, Jupiter Hammon was born at the newly constructed Lloyd family's saltbox manor house. His parents were Rose and Obium, second-generation slaves owned by the master of the house, Henry Lloyd.[1] The manor house was completed just the month prior in September, but it was already bustling with activity as Henry Lloyd had rushed to move his own young family from Boston to the nearly completed manor house in May. Accompanying Henry was his wife, Rebecca, and two young children, Henry II and John. On October 17, the day Hammon was born, there were now three children in the house—John, who was only three months old; Henry, who was two years old; and newborn Jupiter. The close proximity in their ages is important.

In her 2001 essay, "The African-American Poet, Jupiter Hammon: A Home-born Slave and his Classical Name," Margaret A. Brucia explains some key facts about Jupiter Hammon's place in the house and the origin of his name, stating that, "For lack of an equivalent English term, Jupiter was a *verna*, Latin for a home-born slave. Spared the trauma of loss of freedom through abduction, the presumably more malleable and docile *vernae* were highly prized as house slaves in ancient Rome, and they customarily received preferential treatment."[2] Aside from the fervent, heartfelt religiosity displayed in the literary works he produced later in life, loyalty is the only personal quality biographers have attributed to Hammon. But Hammon's early origin hints that the relationships he had within the Lloyd households over eight decades were more complicated than the adjective "loyal" would suggest. It is certain that he received his primary education of reading, writing, and possibly mathematics alongside the other children close to his age within the Lloyd household (Osann 24). He also very likely helped tutor the last two or three of his first master's ten children in his teenage years.[3]

To further contextualize Hammon's childhood, the Lloyd manor house is situated on a fairly remote peninsula connected to the mainland of Long Island by a slender neck of land a quarter of a mile long. The only way on or off the peninsula was either by boat or the narrow, quarter-mile land bridge that connected the peninsula to the mainland. Travel by boat was how the Lloyd family attended St. John's Episcopal Church in Stamford, Connecticut for many years, preferring to attend a congregation with strong ties to the Church of England rather than the local congregational meetinghouses in Huntington. However, most travel would have been by the slender land bridge to the southern side of Lloyd Harbor, toward the town of Huntington. Hammon would have grown up intimately familiar with these waters, roadways, and paths, but ultimately, the Lloyd manor house was a fairly remote location. As a result of this geographical isolation, Hammon would have been among the few playmates available for his master's sons, Henry and John. Five years after Hammon's birth, a third Lloyd child would be added into the mix. Joseph, Henry Lloyd's third child (who would eventually inherit Hammon to become his second master) was born in 1716. Thus, the Lloyd children and Jupiter Hammon (whom we know was highly literate as an adult) would have shared school, play, and the unavoidable hijinks of childhood. These early relationships would, of course, change as Hammon and the Lloyd children grew into teenagers and then adults, but those years would have nevertheless been formative for all involved, and even Hammon's master, Henry Lloyd, seems to have trusted and depended on Hammon far more than any of the other slaves he owned, to whom he generally shows indifference in his letters.[4]

With the recent exceptions of Brucia, Bolton, and Metcalf, commentators of Hammon's works have paid little to no attention to the details of his childhood and upbringing, skipping quickly from his birthdate, which was discovered by Louis Lomax in 1970,[5] to Hammon at age forty-nine when he publishes his first poem, "An Evening Thought," and then focusing strictly on the content of the poetry and prose. There is a reason for this lack of information and context about Hammon's life. Although Jupiter Hammon has been one of the most interesting writers whose career spans the pre-American Revolution through the Post-Revolution periods, he is also one of the most elusive figures when it comes to autobiography or writings about his life story. He rarely wrote directly about himself, and when he did, it was usually within the context of making some important religious point to his readers and listeners. In fact, some early twentieth-century scholars have accused him of evading any reference to his historical moment, choosing to focus his energies on abstract religious ideas. However, this evaluation is based on a faulty structuralist reading of Hammon's works that sought to compare his writings with those of Alexander Pope and John Milton, ignoring the obvious indications that Hammon was engaged in thought about his temporal situation and the historic events unfolding around him—events for which he also had very strong feelings.[6]

In fact, it seems that Hammon had a tremendous amount of interest in themes reflecting his life—even if indirectly—and the events unfolding around him. While it is very difficult to find direct evidence of Hammon's childhood experiences, children and childhood are significant themes in his works. There are numerous references to childhood and children in his 1782 essay, "A Winter Piece," as well as the accompanying poem, "A Poem for Children with Thoughts on Death." He also speaks about the liberation of children from slavery in his 1786 essay, "An Address to the Negroes in the State of New-York." As well, a large proportion of the biblical quotes and paraphrases he uses throughout his works make reference to children and childhood. Arguably, children and childhood preoccupy Hammon as much as spiritual salvation, and perhaps this insight might point readers toward Hammon's sense of his own childhood and experiences in his youth.

Careful reading and contextualization of Hammon within his own time will help us better understand him and his literary themes; it will also clarify specific themes in his writings that have traditionally received little attention by most previous commentators on his life story and art. Students and scholars of Jupiter Hammon and his works already have a wealth of information at their disposal, but there is significant research to be done, too—research that will reveal more materials in seemingly untapped archives that provide further information about Hammon's life and times.

"THAT HE SHOULD BEGIN THE CONFLAGRATION. . . ."

At 1:00 a.m. on the warm, clear morning of Monday, July 5, 1779, a fleet of British ships sailed into the port at New Haven, Connecticut, and set anchor. By the light of a bright half-moon—a half-moon just like the one of Jupiter Hammon's birth in 1711—British General Henry Clinton ordered his commanders to invade and destroy large parts of the city. They were specifically told to destroy any ships in the harbor and then homes, businesses, and supply houses.[7] This move on the part of British forces was meant to draw General George Washington and his Continental Army into direct confrontation and was led by Major General William Tyron. Twelve hours after the initial landing, one of General Tyron's officers, General Garth, reported by dispatch that groups of rebel forces were giving his troops more difficulty than expected and that the town "merits the flames," reporting that he was planning to use the burning of the city as a cover for his forces to rally and continue their march.[8] Ezra Stiles, president of Yale College, watched the landing of the British forces from the steeple of the now nonexistent college chapel. According to his eyewitness account, twenty-four hours after the initial invasion by ground forces, British sailors "came on shore and took their turn at plunder."[9] The weeks that followed were harrowing for the inhabitants of New Haven. No one who was thought by the British forces to be a patriot for the American cause was spared suffering, not even slaves.[10]

There was terrible death, carnage, and suffering in New Haven and throughout the countryside around the city. Some Patriot fighters were tortured before being killed, such as Elisha Tuttle, whose tongue was cut out prior to being executed. However, the stories of battles and the lists of those killed and captured found in traditional histories do not convey the raw fear and terror of those who were caught trying to flee the city while war raged around them. Sarah Lloyd Hillhouse, the wife of one of the Patriot captains leading the defense against the British invaders, writes in a letter of her distress to her aunt, Rebecca Woolsey, stating:

> You who have gone through a like scene can easily imagine the consternation this town must be in on the occasion[.] however we fared much better than we feared as we expected nothing but to see the town reduced to ashes . . . the rest of the inhabitants were plundered & abused without regard to friend of foe—My feelings are not to be described[.] I can only tell you that Mr. Hillhouse was the first that attacked them with a very small party of men with him.[11]

Sarah Hillhouse relates the fear she and her elderly aunt feel as they flee before the British attack force: "Old aunt Lucas and myself rode off when the enemy were within two miles of us[.] the excessive heat of the day together with the fright & above all the distress I felt for my best friends safety had such an effect upon me for some days we were all fearful of the consequences."[12] The "consequences" for Sarah Lloyd Hillhouse personally were, indeed, dire, for in addition to being a young woman caught in the midst of urban warfare, she was also six months pregnant.

This letter is already remarkable for its clear-eyed and frightening firsthand description of the Revolutionary War, a time when many civilians were forced to flee their homes, leaving behind husbands, sons, and brothers to the uncertain fate of a fight against the troops from the world's most powerful army. Sarah also faced the stresses of pregnancy and the uncertainties of the heinous conditions of war. But this letter also goes on to reveal that Jupiter Hammon was present during this violent siege, stating, " . . . [B]ut I am happily reassured & have abundant reason to rejoice in the merciful protection of a kind providence—Our old faithful Jupiter happened to be here & was a great comfort to me in my flight."

Hammon, in 1779, was the property of Sarah's uncle, Joseph Lloyd, who had fled to Connecticut after the British occupation of his home on Long Island. It is uncertain where Joseph Lloyd was during the siege of New Haven, but Sarah's letter—discovered among the Hillhouse Family Papers at Yale University's Manuscripts and Archives of the Sterling Memorial Library—reveals that Jupiter Hammon was present during the invasion, and that the sixty-eight-year-old slave and fellow victim of war had committed himself to protecting and comforting Sarah and her elderly aunt as they navigated through a dangerous landscape consumed by the fires of war.

The information found in Sarah Lloyd Hillhouse's letter helps us to read Jupiter Hammon's own writings with greater context. In particular, it helps us understand how Hammon's religious poetry and essays after 1770 can also be read as *anti-war* literature. July 1779 was a terrible month of fighting in New Haven, and Hammon suffered the violence of war just as his masters did. Those days of conflict clearly shaped the way Jupiter Hammon would think and write about the American War for Independence. Though, as has been discussed, some scholars have suggested that Hammon had nothing to say about the world in which he lived, it is clear from reading his 1783 poem, "A Dialogue, Entitled, The Kind Master and the Dutiful Servant," that he used his wartime experiences in his poetry to express his feelings and ideas about the war and the relationship between masters and slaves, America and the British colonies, God and humanity.

A LINE *on the present* WAR.
SERVANT.
16. Dear Master, now it is a time,
    A time of great distress;
    We'll follow after things divine,
    And pray for happiness.

    MASTER.
17. Then will the happy day appear,
    That virtue shall increase;
    Lay up the sword and drop the spear,
    And nations seek for peace.[13]

The siege at New Haven constitutes the second time Hammon had to flee an invading British force during the course of the war. Hammon was sixty-four years old when the war began and was well into his sixty-eighth year by the time New Haven became a battlefield. For him, the world had abandoned the orderliness he had known for over six decades and descended into—what was for him—a violent and unholy chaos. In November 1779, Hammon would see both Sarah and the daughter she carried die in childbirth. He would also see his second master, Joseph Lloyd, commit suicide the following year as a result of the war. These events and upheavals that befell Hammon's masters materially impacted his own life, particularly as he was quite advanced in age by the standards of the period.

The brief biographies of Hammon that traditionally appear in scholarship have habitually glossed over the events of his life, skipping over moments both monumental and mundane, to deliver a picture of Hammon that falls short of representing him as the complex human being he was. While students, scholars, and general readers can learn much by careful reading of Hammon's poetry and prose, there is still a need to uncover documents that will add further context to his works and perhaps surprise us with new revelations about his life.

The problems of understanding Jupiter Hammon and his writings are twofold: first, the complexities of his thinking have been overshadowed by the perceived notion that he was too accommodating in his thinking about slavery as an institution, though he himself was a slave; and second, his works are habitually dismissed as an overly religious abandonment of the temporal plight of African-American slaves for a simplistic Christian otherworldliness. Even in his own time, his peers accused him of being against the abolition of slavery, though he defended himself by arguing he was indifferent to such matters of temporal concern stating, "I now solemnly declare that I never have said, nor done, any thing [*sic*], neither directly nor indirectly, to promote or to prevent freedom; but my answer hath always been I am a stranger here and I do not care to be concerned or meddle with public affairs . . ." (A Winter Piece 9). However, when looking at the totality of his work, especially alongside his later poem "An Essay on Slavery," it becomes clear that his "indifference" toward the *condition* of being a slave is not the same as his views on the sinfulness of slavery as an *institution*.

Lonnell E. Johnson also writes of Hammon's early, oxymoronic ideas about the ancient Christian concept of slavery and spiritual freedom, a belief influenced by the Pauline epistles regarding slavery but at odds with Hammon's own lived embodiment as "not only a Christian but enslaved in eighteenth-century America" (Johnson 105). Hammon not only embodied this paradox, he struggled mightily in his later years to arrive at a religious philosophy that reconciled his condition as a slave with his personal conviction that slavery was a sin. This, for Hammon, would be a difficult reconciliation given the clear respect he had for his masters and the seemingly mutual affections they shared. To call slavery a sin would be to openly pronounce his masters sinners. I believe that Hammon struggled with, what was for him, a troubling impulse to write his true feelings about slavery without abandoning his own position as a loyal servant to the Lloyd household.

Hammon's earliest known pre-Revolution poem, "An Evening Thought," published as a broadside on Christmas day, 1760, *seems* to be purely religious in content; but even here it is possible to find specific, faint echoes of a slave's complaint and an appeal for mercy in the temporal world of slavery. It is possible "An Evening Thought" is Hammon's first attempt to voice his clear-eyed awareness of the exploitative, explosive political times in which he and his "fellow countrymen" were living—a vision specifically written to express a concern for the Africans and African Americans who constituted his community and for whom he wrote. But Hammon's attitudes about the institution of slavery are far more developed and explicit by 1786, as the newly discovered poem, "An Essay on Slavery," reveals. Discovered in Yale University's archives, among the Hillhouse Family Papers, "An Essay on Slavery" is an explicit condemnation of slavery as an anti-Christian institution to which Hammon (among other enslaved people within his community) wished to see an end. It is an important part of Hammon's canon of works as it helps to show that Hammon was not the apologist for slavery as some may have thought in the past.[14]

HAMMON AND LIBERTY IN CRISIS

In Stanley A. Ransom, Jr.'s 1970 edition of Hammon's works, Vernon Loggins states in one of the introductory essays that

> Perhaps because of his conciliatory attitude toward slavery, Jupiter Hammon's work was disregarded by the earlier Negro leaders, who in most cases kept alive the personalities of their predecessors of any distinction whatsoever. The name of America's first Negro poet dropped into oblivion soon after his death, to remain there for more than a century. (Ransom 41)

Loggins's view of why Jupiter Hammon and his works slipped into near oblivion for more than a century continues to have a residual effect even to the present. And though a number of scholars since the last publication of the Ransom edition of Hammon's works in the 70s and 80s have done exemplary work in

Hammon scholarship—notably Phillip M. Richards, Sondra A. O'Neale, Lonnell E. Johnson, Margaret A. Brucia, and Arlen Nydam—the numbers of students and scholars doing original research on Hammon and his literary works continue to be scant compared to the study of other black writers of the eighteenth and nineteenth centuries. It seems that a general misunderstanding of Hammon's social context has led to this general disinterest in his life and works. It may also be the case that Hammon's writings—the ones readers have had access to sporadically in editions that quickly went out of print and were difficult to obtain—are complex in a way that can easily mislead some readers to draw erroneous conclusions about the value of his literary canon for modern readers.

Today, with the inclusion of the "lost" poems uncovered in the archives since 2011, readers are challenged to rethink some of the previous conclusions about Hammon and his works. When we look at the excerpt from stanza 3 of the recently discovered 1786 Jupiter Hammon poem, "An Essay on Slavery," we can imagine that he was, indeed, not only resigned to his status as slave, but that slavery is, in fact, permissible in the eyes of God.

> When God doth please for to permit
> That slavery should be
> It is our duty to submit
> Till Christ shall make us free

This excerpt seems perfectly consonant with the body of poetry and prose that addressed the issue of slavery written close to the end of Hammon's writing career as we know it. Hammon also writes this fictional exchange between characters in his 1783 poem, "A Dialogue, Entitled, The Kind Master and the Dutiful Servant":

> MASTER.
> 1. COME my servant, follow me,
>   According to thy place;
>   And surely God will be with thee,
>   And send the heav'nly grace.
>
> SERVANT.
> 2. Dear Master, I will follow thee,
>   According to thy word,
>   And pray that God may be with me,
>   And save thee in the Lord.

Taken out of context, these passages might seem to indicate a resignation to the status of slavery Hammon lived in. His most famous piece of writing, his 1787 essay, "An Address to the Negroes of the State of New-York," further seems to confirm this attitude:

> Now I acknowledge that liberty is a great thing, and worth seeking for, if we can get it honestly, and by our good conduct, prevail on our masters to set us free: Though for my own part I do not wish to be free, yet I should be glad, if others, especially the young negroes were to be free, for many of us, who are grown up slaves, and have always had masters to take care of us, should hardly know how to take care of ourselves; and it may be more for our own comfort to remain as we are. That liberty is a great thing we may know from our own feelings, and we may likewise judge so from the conduct of the white-people, in the late war. How much money has been spent, and how many lives have been lost, to defend their liberty ... But this my dear brethren is by no means, the greatest thing we have to be concerned about. Getting our liberty in this world, is nothing to our having the liberty of the children of God. (Hammon 13–14)

So readers of Hammon's works have sometimes been left with the impression that he was too accommodating to the status quo, that he was a "contented" slave. He is also accused of being unaware of his African past, of being indifferent to the sufferings of black people around him. This is a narrow and uninformed way of looking at Hammon's writings.

So what is to be made of Hammon's attitude about his own personal freedom? How does a twenty-first-century readership interpret and understand the poetry and prose of a black writer so different from more familiar and well-studied antebellum models of black male subjectivity representing anti-slavery resistance? Frederick Douglass became the first such model in the popular imagination with his internationally recognized autobiography *A Narrative of the Life of Frederick Douglass,* published in 1845. Douglass, with his struggles for physical, temporal freedom, and his iconic fight with the slave breaker, Covey, has long been the model for a particular mode of black masculinity; one that has, perhaps, served as a litmus test for what would be considered appropriate for inclusion within the canon of antebellum black literature, particularly since the Black Arts/Black Power era when the canon of African-American literature was being established inside and outside of the academy. As politically important as such considerations were in those earlier periods, from the antebellum era through the post-Civil Rights years, entire areas of scholarship and history were left unexplored, areas that would help us understand more clearly what was being faced by enslaved Africans and African Americans of a variety of cultural, regional, and *subject* positions. Frederick Douglass, in his autobiography, for instance, was reflecting on his struggles as a former plantation slave during the prime of his life. Jupiter Hammon, on the other hand, was writing as a literate *elderly* slave reflecting on his current situation and the situation of other members of his slave community. These differences are important. We have few examples of black writers writing about slavery during the time they were enslaved. What Hammon's work offers us is an alternative form of resistant black masculinity, one that is circumscribed by the limitations of his situation and subject position as an enslaved man. If we reject Hammon's works because they do not conform to a preconceived notion of normative black masculinity, we miss out on many of the key nuances and forms of early black thought and resistance to slavery. Hammon's works, because of their keen insights and differences in perspective, reveal some of the deeper problems and struggles faced by enslaved black New Yorkers during and after the American Revolution.

In eighteenth-century New York, for instance, there was a problem whereby masters who had elderly slaves who were beyond their productive laboring years would set those slaves free. These older slaves, though manumitted, were left to fend for themselves, usually without compensation or family to care for them. These slaves, who often could not find employment, usually found themselves indigent, homeless begging in the city streets. Jupiter Hammon, who was seventy-two years old when he wrote "The Kind Master and the Dutiful Servant," and seventy-five years old when he wrote "An Address to the Negroes in the State of New-York," was alluding to the problem of black homelessness and poverty among elderly former slaves who were indifferently manumitted by masters who could no longer profit from their labor. In Hammon's world, manumission for the elderly usually meant spending the last part of their lives homeless and starving. This was such a problem in the state of New York that the state legislature passed a series of laws called "An Act Concerning Slaves" in 1788 (two years after Hammon wrote "An Address"), stipulating that masters who had slaves over the age of fifty who they wished to manumit, either by will or otherwise, would be required to provide financially for those manumitted slaves by providing the municipality the new freeperson was to live in with a bond of no less than two hundred pounds.[15] Thus, the system of chattel slavery contributed directly to, and set the preconditions for, black poverty and homelessness in the state of New York. Hammon's poem and then his later essay represent, therefore, a compromise between the master and the enslaved person, a compromise setting out what Hammon perceived to be the most ethical relationship that could be between a master and his property, an enslaved human being like himself. At a time when there were no laws to protect elderly slaves from being rendered homeless at the whim of their masters, Hammon chose to outline a compromise, a pragmatic path to some degree of security, not only for himself, but for other elderly slaves living within his community. "The Kind Master and the Dutiful Servant" is not a capitulation to slavery, but rather a document that expresses the anxiety felt by enslaved peoples whose futures were determined by the whims of masters concerned with commerce and the profit their slaves would bring them. Hammon uses religion and religious ethics to mediate the damage the system of chattel slavery has inflicted on the lives of black people by pointing at a set of duties and relationships that Christianity demands from its practitioners.

The introduction of "An Essay on Slavery" to Hammon's body of work fills an important critical gap in our understanding of Hammon's complicated and evolving ideas concerning slavery. It is important to note that "An Essay on Slavery" was written in the same year and completed around the same time as Hammon's "An Address to the Negroes of the State of New-York." While the two works agree on the issue of God's *permission* for slavery to exist in America, the unpublished "Essay on Slavery" goes much further than "An Address" in the way it handles the morality of slave-keeping. By all measures, it is Hammon's boldest argument *against* slavery as an institution endorsed by God. This distinction is crucial; whereas "An Address" seems more conciliatory toward the institution itself, suggesting some form of gradual emancipation is necessary to bring chattel slavery to an end, "An Essay on Slavery" paints the institution as universally despised by both slaves and God.

In the first stanza, Hammon acknowledges, with some sense of pride, the origins of African peoples living in America:

I
Our forefathers came from Africa
tost over the raging main
to a Christian shore for there to stay
and not return again
          ("Essay on Slavery")

His reference to forefathers is a reverent one, and their presence in the New World is highlighted by the fact that they survived "the raging main" or, rather, the Middle Passage. Among those forefathers, Hammon is certainly counting women, as this stanza is a combination of images drawn from two stanzas of his 1778 poem, "An Address to Miss Phillis Wheatley":

4.
God's tender mercy brought thee here,
Tost o'er the raging main;   Psal. ciii. 1. 2, 3, 4.
In Christian faith thou hast a share,
Worth all the gold of Spain.

5.
While thousands tossed by the sea,
And others settled down,   Death.
God's tender mercy set thee free,
From dangers still unknown.
    ("Address to Miss Phillis Wheatley")

The similarities in language, style, meter, and imagery are apparent between these stanzas of the two poems. Both poems have sections that address, quite directly, the Middle Passage, and both pay homage to those who died in the brutal exchange across continents. Additionally, though the voyage was deadly, it was nevertheless fortuitous for those who survived the trip, for they now would have the benefit of being instructed in Christianity. Hammon shares this sentiment with Phillis Wheatley, who wrote similarly in her poem, "On Being Brought from Africa to America":

'Twas mercy brought me from my *Pagan* land,
Taught my benighted soul to understand
That there's a God, that there's a *Savior* too:
Once I redemption neither sought nor knew.
    ("On Being Brought from Africa to America")

It is very likely that Hammon is explicitly elaborating on Wheatley's short 1773 poem, extending her personal relief at salvation into a celebration of their shared heritage with a larger body of African peoples, as well as celebrating entrance into the Christian tradition. The Middle Passage figures large in both his poems, and the dangers of the voyage are highlighted. Notice that the marginal note "death" is the only descriptive reference that is not a bible passage in this poem. Death figures large in all of Hammon's writings, particularly its imminence. This is something that Wheatley does not do in her poem. It is very possible that Hammon, through a poetic persona, is acting as a mentor figure for Wheatley as they engage in a dialogue through their poetry. Hammon's (re)visioning of Wheatley's narrative (particularly as she, herself, survived the Middle Passage as a child) reveals a self-conscious effort to connect with their shared

African heritage and celebrate both survival and the grace of God in the face of imminent death.

But Hammon is also doing something subtler and theologically relevant in his "Address to Miss Phillis Wheatley"; he is writing himself and all other African-descended slaves in America into a shared biblical history. Each stanza is accompanied by a biblical passage, and that passage parallels the experiences and desires related in each stanza of his poem. So, here we have a clue that Hammon sees his life, and the lives of the people around him, as the continuation of Christian history, that he, as well as other African slaves, are a part of an ongoing Christian narrative. Hammon's effort to write African-descended American slaves into the ongoing Christian narrative becomes a priority in his writings. This being the case, his poetry and prose must be read with an eye toward his literal belief.

Given the apparent close connection stylistically and ideologically between Hammon's earlier works, and his "Essay on Slavery," the second stanza reveals to us, far more explicitly than ever before, Hammon's *religious* view of the institution of slavery:

2
Dark and dismal was the Day
When slavery began
All humble thoughts were put away
Then slaves were made by Man
           ("Essay on Slavery")

Nowhere in Jupiter Hammon's writings does he make so stark and plain a negative statement about the institution of slavery and its denigration of humanity. In "A Dialogue, Entitled, The Kind Master and the Dutiful Servant," the image of slavery *seems* to be represented in an idyllic fashion. For instance:

    MASTER.
3. My Servant, lovely is the Lord,
   And blest those servants be,
   That truly love his holy word,
   And thus will follow me.

    SERVANT.
4. Dear Master, that's my whole delight,
   Thy pleasure for to do;
   As far as grace and truth's in sight,
   Thus far I'll surely go.

But contrast the above stanzas with stanzas two and three of "An Essay on Slavery":

2

Dark and dismal was the Day
When slavery began
All humble thoughts were put away
Then slaves were made by Man.

3

When God doth please for to permit
That slavery should be
It is our duty to submit
Till Christ shall make us free

The passages *seem* to contradict each other, but this is not the case given Hammon's complicated theological perspective: though slavery is a man-made sin, he is bound by God to nevertheless endure his servitude as pronounced by the apostle Paul (Ephesians 6:5–8, Colossians 3:22–25, 1 Timothy 6:1, Titus 2:9–10, 1 Peter 2:18–25). But it is in Hammon's use of 1 Peter 2:18–25 and Philemon 13–17 that we begin to understand how Hammon can reconcile a sinful slavery with obedience to God. The mandate to obedience is so that the slave may serve as an example of righteousness, suffering for the wrongs inflicted against him on Earth, just as Jesus served as an example to suffer crucifixion to save a sinful humanity.

Thus, the suffering of the Middle Passage that Hammon highlights in two poems symbolizes the unjust suffering of slaves at the hands of their masters. And though there may be so-called "good" masters, they are nevertheless the creators of slavery, sinners to be ministered to, and for Hammon, equal brothers who must be brought back to righteousness through the example of long-suffering servitude. It is a difficult, hard theology, but one that is consonant with Paul's repeated mandate for slaves to be loyal to their masters while allowing slaves, such as Hammon, to equate the *institution* with sin.

Without this new poem, "Essay on Slavery," it is difficult to arrive at this fuller understanding of Hammon's beliefs about slavery, that he can both despise it and submit to it as part of a genuine, heartfelt belief that he finally arrives at as the righteous path for him. Hammon completed "An Essay on Slavery" in 1786, the same year he wrote "An Address to the Negroes of the State of New-York," which he presented to the members of the African Society in the city of New York in September. The essay was later printed and published in New York in February 1787. But there is an interesting convergence of dates between the completion of these two documents. The handwritten draft of "An Essay on Slavery" is dated November 19, 1786, after "An Address to the Negroes" was completed, but before it was published. I argue that, since Jupiter Hammon's other two essays ended with a poem, he intended "An Essay on Slavery" to be published along with "An Address to the Negroes of the State of New-York."

"A Winter Piece" and "An Evening Thought" each have an accompanying poem at the end of the text, "A Poem For Children, with Thoughts on Death," and "A Dialogue, Entitled, The Kind Master and the Dutiful Servant," respectively. A truer presentation of "An Address to the Negroes of the State of New-York," the presentation intended by Hammon, would have included "An Essay on Slavery" at the end of the essay. This reconstruction of the text significantly changes the tone and scope of "An Address," and it certainly would have changed the way generations of readers responded to the text of the essay. It is not definitively known yet why "An Essay on Slavery" was not included with "An Address" in the essay's original 1787 publication. This edition of Hammon's known works juxtaposes "An Address to the Negroes of the State of New-York" with "An Essay on Slavery" to reconstruct a text more in line with what I believe to be Hammon's original vision.

While most readers approach Hammon from the perspective of either religion or what he has to say about liberty within the context of slavery, the discovery of his 1770 poem, "Dear Hutchinson is Dead and Gone,"[16] indicates that he was also concerned with matters of *religious* liberty. But another aspect of this newly discovered 1770 poem that deserves immediate attention is how similar it is in language, structure, and tone to Hammon's well-known poem, "An Address to Miss Phillis Wheatley." The first stanza of "Dear Hutchinson" reads,

O Come Ye youth of Boston town
The mournfull News youl hear
The pious youth though just come on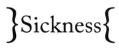
Shall Quickly Disappear

While the first stanza of "An Address to Miss Phillis Wheatley" reads,

O Come you pious youth! adore
    The wisdom of thy God,   Eccles. xii. 1.
In bringing thee from distant shore,
    To learn his holy word.

The opening stanzas of these two poems bear striking similarities that continue throughout each. They are both encomiums to women of Boston, one woman a persecuted religious dissident, the other a slave and poet, just like Hammon.

While it is not possible at this time to know exactly when "Dear Hutchinson is Dead and Gone" was written, we do know it was originally composed eight years before "An Address to Miss Phillis Wheatley," making it possible that Hammon used "Dear Hutchinson" as the template for his celebratory encomium to Phillis Wheatley. The text of "Dear Hutchinson" that appears in this edition is transcribed from a copy of the original source text made during Hammon's life. Hammon's original text has been lost, but a copy of the text, made by Phebe Townsend during Hammon's lifetime, survives so that readers and scholars today have knowledge and access to this lost Hammon poem. Phebe Townsend was a member of a prominent New England family who were acquaintances of the Lloyd family. Townsend's copy of this poem by Hammon indicates that he circulated his unpublished written works outside of the Lloyd households, perhaps giving modern readers and researchers clues about potential literary circles or reading groups he may have participated in. Since the source text we have today is a copy of the original, it is difficult to determine which variations in spelling and grammar belong to Hammon and which are transcription mistakes made by Townsend. The eleventh stanza of the poem, which is struck through, was an obvious transcription error by Phebe Townsend, as she clearly lost track of where she was reading as she copied Hammon's original text. This edition reproduces the Phebe Townsend copy of the Hammon poem to allow modern readers and researcher to study and consider the structural nuances of the poem as they appear in the original, hand-copied source that exists in the Library of the New-York Historical Society.

In the way of primary materials representing Jupiter Hammon's known works, we currently have three essays and, with the recent discoveries of "An Essay on Slavery" and "Dear Hutchinson is Dead and Gone," we have six complete poems. It is known that Hammon wrote at least one more poem entitled "An Essay on the Ten Virgins" that has yet to be discovered, and to the present, no one has identified any of his *non-literary* writing. It is known that Hammon was trusted with helping conduct the business of the Lloyd family, so it is highly likely that he kept lists, records, and other documents in addition to his literary writing containing handwriting that could be compared against the manuscripts we now have. An examination of Hammon's handwriting shows that he was very skilled with a quill pen, especially compared with some of the less-readable writing of other members of the Lloyd and Hillhouse households. It is therefore quite possible that within the archives of these families, there could be some remnant of Hammon's non-literary writing. These writings would reveal much about him as a member of the Lloyd household, as well as the larger communities of Queens

Village and New Haven. These documents, and other literary writing, set the stage for exciting, new, additional in-depth research.

NOTES

1. See Bolton and Metcalf, "The Migration of Jupiter Hammon and His Family: From Slavery to Freedom and its Consequences," *Long Island History Journal*, lihj.cc.stonybrook.edu/2013 /articles/the-migration-of-jupiter-hammon-and-his-family-from-slavery-to-freedom-and-its -consequences/, paragraphs 12–13.

2. See Brucia, "The African-American Poet, Jupiter Hammon: A Home-born Slave and his Classical Name." *International Journal of the Classical Tradition*, vol. 7, no. 4, 2001, 515–22.

3. Henry Lloyd was Jupiter Hammon's first master. Of Henry Lloyd's ten children, Hammon would see two die in their early thirties, and the youngest of the Lloyd's children, James Lloyd, would be forced to flee America and immigrate to London because of his loyalty to the British government during the American Revolution.

4. Various letters in the two-volume *Papers of the Lloyd Family of the Manor of Queen's Village, Lloyd's Neck, Long Island, New York, 1654–1826* (1926–27) reveal that Henry Lloyd, Sr., was in no way sentimental in his relationships with the slaves he owned and was impatient with the free people of color who lived on Long Island. Henry Lloyd bought and sold enslaved Africans and African Americans for himself and as an intermediary for others in his community.

5. See "Notes on First Black Poet" in *The Afro-American*, no. 35, April 18, 1970.

6. Stanley A. Ransom, Jr., edited the most important twentieth-century edition of Jupiter Hammon's works, *America's First Negro Poet: The Complete Works of Jupiter Hammon of Long Island* (1970), and he was an active advocate for Hammon's legacy as a writer, but his edition opens with essays by Oscar Wegelin and Vernon Loggins, both of whom make claims about the dearth of historical references within Hammon's works, as well as remarking that his poetry and prose lack significantly as art, relegating Hammon's work to—in Loggins's estimation—"folk poetry" (37). Wegelin accuses Hammon, as a thinker and writer, of being, "tinged with narrowness and superstition" (30), while Loggins claims that Hammon's "Mystic Negro mind" (37) played with notions of religion in his art. Even when these commentators find merit in Hammon's writing, their comments are mediated by qualifications such as Wegelin's statement about Hammon's poetry that, "Although grammatically almost perfect, it seems certain that an abler and more experienced hand than his own was responsible for this" (30). Wegelin offers no evidence for this, and as readers will observe in this new edition of Hammon's works, it may be the case that the printers and other intermediaries of the time *may* have actually introduced mistakes into Hammon's printed works. Without a doubt, the Ransom edition was extremely important in keeping Hammon's legacy as a writer alive, and while Wegelin and Loggins probably believed they were being objective—and perhaps even a bit progressive in their commentaries—it is arguable that readers' perceptions of Hammon's works have been negatively influenced by opening essays that imposed racist ideologies of black inferiority on Jupiter Hammon's texts. This new edition attempts to correct this error for twenty-first-century readers.

7. See *The British Invasion of New Haven, Connecticut: Together with Some Account of Their Landing and Burning The Towns of Fairfield and Norwalk, July 1779* (1879), 33–34.

8. Townshend, Charles 40.

9. Townshend 41–42. This is an eyewitness account by Ezra Stiles, who stayed as long as possible so he could oversee the evacuation of his family and the important papers of Yale College. Townshend gets this eyewitness account from Ezra Stiles's diary recounting the event.

10. Townshend 22. Townshend lists free blacks and slaves as among the killed, wounded, and captured during the siege. See *The British Invasion of New Haven* (1879).

11. Hillhouse, Sarah Lloyd. "New Haven, July 19th, 1779." Letter to Rebecca Woolsey. 19 July 1779. Yale University Archives, New Haven. Manuscript.

12. Ibid.

13. For an in-depth analysis of "The Kind Master and the Dutiful Servant," see *Evangelism and Resistance in the Black Atlantic, 1760–1835* (2008), 40–42.

14. See May and McCown, "'An Essay on Slavery': An Unpublished Poem by Jupiter Hammon." *Early American Literature*, vol. 48, no. 2, 2013, 457–71.

15. See Thomas Greenleaf, printer, *Laws of the State of New York, Comprising the Constitution and Acts of Legislature, Since the Revolution, From the First to the Fifteenth Sessions, Inclusive*, vol. 2, 1792, 85–88.

16. The poem "Dear Hutchinson is Dead and Gone" was discovered in November 2014 by Claire Bellerjeau. See "Researcher Discovers New Poem by Jupiter Hammon, Slave from Lloyd Harbor," *Newsday*. March 2, 2015, www.newsday.com/long-island/history/claire-bellerjeau-researcher-discovers-new-poem-by-jupiter-hammon-slave-from-lloyd-harbor-1.10000707.

THE COLLECTED WORKS OF JUPITER HAMMON

AN
Evening THOUGHT.
SALVATION BY *CHRIST*,
WITH
PENETENTIAL[1] CRIES:

Composed by Jupiter Hammon, a Negro belonging to Mr Lloyd, of Queen's-
Village, on Long-Island, the 25th of December, 1760.

SALVATION comes by Jesus Christ alone,
    The only Son of God;
Redemption now to every one,
    That love his holy Word.
Dear Jesus we would fly to Thee,
    And leave off every Sin,
Thy tender Mercy well agree;
    Salvation from our King.
Salvation comes now from the Lord,
    Our victorious King;
His holy Name be well ador'd,
    Salvation surely bring.
Dear Jesus give thy Spirit now,
    Thy Grace to every Nation,
That han't the Lord to whom we bow,
    The Author of Salvation.
Dear Jesus unto Thee we cry,
    Give us thy Preparation;
Turn not away thy tender Eye;
    We seek thy true Salvation.
Salvation comes from God we know,
    The true and only One;
It's well agreed and certain true,
    He gave his only Son.
Lord hear our penetential Cry:
    Salvation from above;

Lord turn our dark benighted Souls;
    Give us a true Motion,[2]
And let the Hearts of all the World,
    Make Christ their Salvation.
Ten Thousand[3] Angels cry to Thee,
    Yea louder than the Ocean.
Thou art the Lord, we plainly see;
    Thou art the true Salvation.
Now is the Day, excepted Time;
    The Day of Salvation;
Increase your Faith, do not repine:
    Awake ye every Nation.
Lord unto whom now shall we go,
    Or seek a safe Abode;
Thou hast the Word Salvation too
    The only Son of God.
Ho! every one that hunger hath,[4]
    Or pineth after me,
Salvation be thy leading Staff,
    To set the Sinner free.
Dear Jesus unto Thee we fly;
    Depart, depart from Sin,
Salvation doth at length supply,
    The Glory of our King.
Come ye Blessed of the Lord,
    Salvation gently given;

[*left column continued on p. 2*]

[*right column continued on p. 2*]

1

It is the Lord that doth supply,
  With his Redeeming Love.
Dear Jesus by thy precious Blood,
  The World Redemption have:
Salvation comes now from the Lord,
  He being thy captive Slave.
Dear Jesus let the Nations cry,
  And all the People say,
Salvation comes from Christ on high,
  Haste on Tribunal Day.
We cry as Sinners to the Lord,
  Salvation to obtain;
It is firmly fixt his holy Word,
  Ye shall not cry in vain.
Dear Jesus unto Thee we cry,
  And make our Lamentation:
O let our Prayers ascend on high;
  We felt thy Salvation.

[*right column begins on p. 1*]

O turn your Hearts, accept the Word,
  Your Souls are fit for Heaven.
Dear Jesus we now turn to Thee,
  Salvation to obtain;
Our Hearts and Souls do meet again,
  To magnify thy Name.
Come holy spirit, Heavenly Dove,
  The Object of our Care;
Salvation doth increase our Love;
  Our Hearts hath felt thy fear.
Now Glory be to God on High,
  Salvation high and low;
And thus the Soul on Christ rely,
  To Heaven surely go.
Come Blessed Jesus, Heavenly Dove,
  Accept Repentance here;
Salvation give, with tender Love;
  Let us with Angels share.

FINIS.

NOTES

1. Hammon's spelling of the word "penitential" appears to be a common variant of the word during his lifetime. The same spelling may be found in several texts, including the fourth edition of the popular poetry collection, *The Beauties of the Poets: Being a Collection of Moral and Sacred Poetry, From the Most Eminent Authors*, 1792. This particular collection contains an excerpt from Book 10 of John Milton's *Paradise Lost*, lines 720–834, and lists the excerpt as "Adam's Penetential Reflections After The Fall." I was not able to find an earlier edition of this collection, though later editions modernize the spelling of "penetential" to "penitential." Though Milton does use the word "penitent" in Books 10 and 12, he never uses any variant of the word "penitential."

2. Hammon is making a comparison between the motion of the planets and other heavenly bodies similar to the way eighteenth-century natural philosophers would have imagined them, as well as the motion by which a Christian god moves the human soul.

3. The number "ten thousand" is used numerous times throughout the Bible, usually signifying a number of armed soldiers.

4. This line is an allusion to Isaiah 49:10, "They shall not hunger nor thirst; neither shall the heat nor sun smite them: for he that hath mercy on them shall lead them, even by the springs of the water shall he guide them." In this passage, God is renewing His covenant with the Jewish diaspora but, in context, it can also be read as an allusion to the future ministry of Jesus.

DEAR HUTCHINSON IS DEAD AND GONE[1]

O Come Ye youth of Boston town
The mournfull News youl hear[2]
The pious youth though just come on
Shall Quickly Disappear

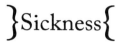

She Always did appear to be
A chosen child of god
he gave her grace that set her free
she loved his holy word

In Wisdoms ways she always went
or gave a just Record
for Every sin she should Repent
And fly unto the Lord

She like a lamb or mournful dove
She silently did cry
Dear Jesus Come ye from above
My Soul on the Rely

She did confirm the Holy word
to youth that live in sin
to leave that way and Serve the Lord
that Christ may take them in

She going the way of all the Earth
her Nature doth Decay
Dear Jesus send her thy Relief
And help her now to pray

Not many days before the word
her panting heart did fly
She thus prayed unto the Lord
And met a fresh Reply

Come Blessed Jesus now look down
have mercy on my soul
and thus forgive the Ills i've Done
and Quickly send thy Call

Soon after setting of the sun
that ruler of the day
God sent his greatfull summons down
to fleet her soul away

Death

Shes gone were all Gods Children are
Shes gone from us tis true
Shes gone to Christ were angels share
and bid the world adieu

~~Soon after setting of the sun~~
~~that ruler of the day~~
~~God sent his greatful summons down~~[3]

this Blessed youth hath sen the day
that Nations fear to try
the Lord hath fetch her soul away
to taste Eternity

twas from the dust at the first word
yea from the Earth she Came
And to the dust though in the Lord
Go Earth to Earth again[4]

She is past the glomy vail of Death
Recievd that Blessed Call
Where angels stand for to attest
Admittanc to her soul

While parents stood with Drooping head
his tears ran Dreeping Down
Blest angels did perfume the Bed
he stood with Glory Crown

Why should ye mourn ye Parent Now
Why should your heart Repine
With holy Job with Whom ye Vow
be always of that mind

Twas God that gave our Pious one
tis God that takes away
twas God that sent his summons Down
to taste Eternal day

the mournful Bell Begins to tole   { funeral
to trace her to the ground
Dear Jesus doth Possess her soul
though we have felt the wound

Come ye mourners now and see
the place of her abode
turn dust to Dust and let it Be
She sleepeth in the Lord

Dear Hutchinson is dead and gone
And Left a Memorial
And as a Child that is New born
She Loved Gods Holy wil

Now Glory be unto the Lord
an Blessed be his Name
Come follow now his holy word
Until you meet again

Composed by Jupiter hammon
A Negro Belonging to mr Joseph Lloyd
Of Queens Village on Long island
August the 10th 1770

Phebe Townsend

NOTES

1. The poem is written on a single large sheet of laid paper, folded into halves. The first thirty lines are written on one half of one side of the sheet, and the rest of the poem is written on the two halves of the other side of the paper. The poem is a copy of Jupiter Hammon's original, transcribed by Phebe Townsend, whose family was acquaintances with the Lloyd family. The title "Dear Hutchinson is Dead and Gone" is taken from the seventy-sixth line of the untitled poem copied in Phebe Townsend's hand. The original line does not capitalize the "d" and "g" (for the words "dead" and "gone"), but I capitalize them in this volume to indicate the line's use as a title for the poem, indicating the composition's subject.

2. Hammon included the marginal annotation "Death" in this stanza similar to the marginal annotations he places in his poem, "An Address to Miss Phillis Weatley."

3. Phebe Townsend mistakenly begins recopying the thirty-first stanza after the thirty-second one, and then strikes out the repeated lines when she realizes her error. Readers should notice that she spells the word "grateful" differently here (with only one letter "l") than in the original thirty-first stanza.

4. This passage is a paraphrase of the section on the burial of the dead from the *Book of Common Prayer*: "Forasmuch as it hath pleased Almighty God in his wise Providence to take out of this world the soul of our deceased *brother* lying now before us, we therefore commit *his* Body to the ground; earth to earth, ashes to ashes, dust to dust" (the 1789 edition, printed in Philadelphia for the Protestant Episcopal Church 285).

Come All ye youth of Boston town
the mournfull News youl hear
the Pious youth though Just come on
Shall Quickly Disappear

She Always did appear to be
A Chosen Child of god
he Gave her Grace that Set her free
She Lovd his holy Word

In Wisdoms ways She always went
or Gave a Just Record
for Every Sin She Should Repent
And fly unto the Lord

She Like a Lamb to mournfull days
She Silently did Cry
Dear Jesus Come ye from above
My Soul on the high

She did Confirm the Holy word
to youth that Live in Sin
to Leave that way and Serve the Lord
that Christ may take them in

She Going the way of all the Earth
her Nature doth Decay
Dear Jesus Send her thy Relief
And help her now to Pray

Not many days before the word
her fainting heart did fly afresh
She thus Prayed unto the Lord
And met afresh Reply

Come Blessed Jesus now Look down
have mercy on my Soul
and thus forgive the Sins I done
and Quickly Send thy Call

Soon after setteing of the Sun   Death
that ruler of the day
God Sent his Greatfull Summons down
to flet her Soul away

Shes gone were all gods Children are Ifly
Shes gone from us tis true
Shes gone to Christ were angels Shaire
and bid the world adieu

~~Soon after setting of the Sune~~
~~that ruler of the day~~
~~God Sent his Greatful Summons down~~

this Blessed youth hath sen the day
that Nations fear to try ~~~~
the Lord hath fetch her Soul away
to taste Eternity

teas from the dust at the first word
you from the Earth She came
And to the dust though in the Lord
Go Earth to Earth again

She is Past the Glomy vail of Death
Recieved that Blessed pell
Where angels Stand for to attest
Admittanc to her Soul

While Parents Stood with Drooping head
his tears ran Dreeping down
Blest angels did perfume the Bed
he Soul with Glory Crown

Why Should ye mourn ye Parent Now
Why Should your heart Repine
With holy Job with whom ye ows
be away of that mind

'Twas God that gave our Pleasure once
'tis God that takes away
'tis God that sent his Summons Down
Taste Eternal day

The mournful Bell Begins to tole   } funeral
To trace her to the ground
Dear Jesus doth Possess her Soul
though we have felt the wound

Come ye mourners now and Se
the Place of her abode
turn dust to Dust and Let it Be
She Sleepeth in the Lord

Dear Hutchinson is dead and Gone
and Left a Memorial
and as a Child that is New born
She Said God's holy will

Now Glory be unto the Lord
an Blessed be his Name
Come follow now his holy word
until you meet again

Composed by Jupiter hammon
A Negro Belonging to mr Joseph lloyd
of Quens Village on Long island
August the 10th 1770

Phebe Townsend

HARTFORD, AUGUST 4, 1778

AN ADDRESS to Miss **PHILLIS WHEATLEY**, Ethiopian Poetess,
in Boston, who came from Africa at eight years of age, and
soon became acquainted with the gospel of Jesus Christ.

Miss **WHEATLEY**, pray give me leave to express as follows:

1.
O Come you pious youth! adore
The wisdom of thy God, Eccles. xii. 1.
In bringing thee from distant shore,
To learn his holy word.

2.
Thou mightst been left behind,
Amidst a dark abode; Psal. cxxxvi. 1, 2, 3.
God's tender mercy still combin'd,
Thou hast the holy word.

3.
Fair wisdom's ways are paths of peace,
And they that walk therein, Psal. i. 1, 2, 3.
Shall reap the joys that never cease,
       Prov. iii. 7.
And Christ shall be their king.

4.
God's tender mercy brought thee here,
Tost o'er the raging main; Psal. ciii. 1, 2, 3, 4.
In Christian faith thou hast a share,
Worth all the gold of Spain.

5.
While thousands tossed by the sea,
And others settled down, Death.

Among the heathen live no more,
Come magnify thy God.

12.
I pray the living God may be,
The shepherd of thy soul; Psal. lxxx. 1, 2, 3.
His tender mercies still are free,
His mysteries to unfold.

13.
Thou, Phillis, when thou hunger hast,
Or pantest for thy God; Psal. xlii. 1, 2, 3.
Jesus Christ is thy relief,
Thou hast the holy word.

14.
The bounteous mercies of the Lord,
Are hid beyond the sky, Psal. xvi. 10, 11.
And holy souls that love his word,
Shall taste them when they die.

15.
These bounteous mercies are from God,
The merits of his Son; Psal. xxxiv. 19.
The humble soul that loves his word,
He chooses for his own.

[*left column continued on p. 12*]

[*right column continued on p. 12*]

God's tender mercy set thee free,
From dangers still unknown.

6.

That thou a pattern still might be,
To youth of Boston town,   2 Cor. v. 10.
The blessed Jesus set thee free,
From every sinful wound.

7.

The blessed Jesus, who came down,
Unvail'd his sacred face,   Rom. v. 21.
To cleanse the soul of every wound,
And give repenting grace.

8.

That we poor sinners may obtain
The pardon of our sin;   Psal. xxxiv. 6, 7, 8.
Dear blessed Jesus now constrain,
And bring us flocking in.

9.

Come you, Phillis, now aspire,
And seek the living God,   Matth. vii. 7, 8.
So step by step thou mayst go higher,
Till perfect in the word.

10.

While thousands mov'd to distant shore,
And others left behind,   Psal. lxxxix. 1.
The blessed Jesus still adore,
Implant this in thy mind.

11.

Thou hast left the heathen shore,

          Psal. xxxiv. 1, 2, 3.

Thro' mercy of the Lord;

[*right column begins on p. 11*]

16.

Come, dear Phillis, be advis'd,
To drink Samarias' flood;   John iv. 13, 14.
There nothing is that shall suffice,
But Christ's redeeming blood.

17.

While thousands muse with earthly toys,
And range about the street,   Matth. vi. 33.[1]
Dear Phillis, seek for heaven's joys,
Where we do hope to meet.

18.

When God shall send his summons
down,
And number saints together,   Psal. cxvi. 19.
Blest angels chant, (triumphant sound)
Come live with me for ever.

19.

The humble soul shall fly to God,
And leave the things of time,   Mat. v. 3, 8.
Start forth as 'twere at the first word,
To taste things more divine.

20.

Behold! the soul shall wast[2] away,
Whene'er we come to die,   Cor. xv. 51, 52, 53.[3]
And leave its cottage made of clay,
In twinkling of an eye.

21.

Now glory be to the Most High,
United praises given,   Psal. cl. 6.
By all on earth, incessantly,
And all the host of heav'n.

Composed by JUPITER HAMMON, a Negro Man belonging to Mr. JOSEPH
LLOYD, of Queen's Village, on Long-Island, now in Hartford.

* * *The above lines are published by the Author, and a number of his friends, who desire
to join with him in their best regards to Miss WHEATLEY.

1. This section of the sermon is a part of the cycle of sayings commonly referred to as "The Sermon on the Mount," which contrasts the evils of pursuing earthly wealth and physical well-being with the pursuit of spiritual wealth, a wealth attained by concentrating on the singular lived moment and contemplation of God. This part of the cycle is also the location from which Hammon paraphrases the sentence, "Ye cannot serve God and mammon" (Matthew 5:24), which he also uses in the twenty-fifth stanza of his poem, "A Dialogue, Entitled, The Kind Master and the Dutiful Servant." Matthew 5:19–34 contains what appears to be some of Hammon's favorite biblical verses, as he often quotes from this section of the Bible.

2. The word "waste." The original spelling is retained here.

3. Hammon is specifically referencing 1 Corinthians 15:51–53. The book is not noted in the original text.

AN ESSAY ON THE TEN VIRGINS

"An Essay on the Ten Virgins" is a poem by Jupiter Hammon that has not yet been discovered. There are no known copies of the poem; however, it was advertised in the December 14, 1779, edition of the *Connecticut Courant*, suggesting the poem was written during the American Revolution when Hammon was living in Hartford, Connecticut, with his master, Joseph Lloyd.

To be sold at the Printing Office in Hartford,

An Essay on the Ten Virgins.

Composed by JUPITER HAMMON.
a Negro Man belonging to MR. JOSEPH LLOYD of
Queen's Village Long Island, Now in Hartford.

1779 was a difficult year for the family that Jupiter Hammon served. In July 1779, Hammon was in New Haven, Connecticut, where he was tasked with protecting Sarah Lloyd Hillhouse—Joseph Lloyd's niece—while British forces sacked and burned the city around them. Sarah had married James Hillhouse in January of that year and was six months' pregnant at the time of the siege in July. In October, Sarah died during childbirth and her baby, also named Sarah, died the next morning. Hammon was likely affected by all of the violence and death around him that the war had brought. I believe that though his poem "An Essay on the Ten Virgins" was likely an extended paraphrase of the Book of Matthew 25:1–13, I also believe the poem will incorporate an anti-war sentiment into its lessons about the preparations for the coming of death, both of which were pre-occupations within Hammon's poetry and prose after 1778.

A
WINTER PIECE:
BEING A
SERIOUS EXHORTATION,
WITH A CALL TO THE
UNCONVERTED:
AND A SHORT
CONTEMPLATION
ON THE
DEATH OF JESUS CHRIST.
WRITTEN BY
JUPITER HAMMON,

A **NEGRO MAN** belonging to Mr. John Lloyd, of

Queen's Village, on Long Island, now in Hartford.

Published by the AUTHOR with the Assistance

Of his Friends

HARTFORD:

PRINTED FOR THE **AUTHOR**.

M.DCC.LXXXII.[1]

A SERIOUS EXHORTATION, &c.

As I have been desired to write something more than Poetry, I shall endeavour to write from these words, Matthew xi, 28. *Come unto me all ye that labour and are heavy laden.*

My Brethren, I shall endeavour by divine assistance, to shew what is meant by coming to the Lord Jesus Christ labouring and heavy laden, and to conclude, I shall contemplate on the death of Jesus Christ.

My Brethren, in the first place, I am to shew what is meant by coming to Christ labouring and heavy laden. We are to come with a sense of our own unworthiness, and to confess our sins before the most high God, and to come by prayer and meditation, and we are to confess Christ to be our Saviour and mighty Redeemer. Matthew x, 33. *Whosoever shall confess me before men, him will I confess before my heavenly father.*[2] Here, my brethren, we have great encouragement to come to the Lord and ask for the influence of his holy spirit, and that he would give us the water of eternal life, John iv.14. Whosoever shall drink of this water as the woman of Samaria[3] did, shall never thirst; but it shall be in them a well of water springing up to eternal life, then we shall believe in the merits of Christ, for our eternal salvation, and come labouring and heavy laden with a sense of our lost and undone state without an interest in the merits of Christ. It should be our greatest care to trust in the Lord, as David did, Psalm xxxi, I. *In thee O Lord put I my trust.*[4]

My Brethren, we must come to the divine fountain to turn us from sin to holiness, and to give us grace to repent of all our sins; this none can do but God. We must come labouring and heavy laden not trusting to our own righteousness, but we are to be cloathed [*sic*] with the righteousness of Christ. Then may we apply this text, Psalm xxxiii, 7. *Blessed is he whose transgressions is forgiven, whose sins, is covered.*[5] This we must seek for by prayer and meditation, and we are to pray without ceasing, and the word is set forth by David in Psalm lxi, I. *Have mercy on me O God, according to thy loving kindness, according unto the multitude of thy tender mercies blot out my transgressions.*[6] My Brethren we are to come poor in spirit.

In the second place in order to come to the divine fountain labouring and heavy laden, we are to avoid all bad company, to keep ourselves pure in heart.

Matthew v. 8. *Blessed are the poor in heart for they shall see God.*[7] Now, in order to see God we must have a saving change wrought in our hearts, which is the work of God's holy spirit which we are to ask for, Matthew vii, 7. *Ask and it shall be given you, seek and ye shall find.* It may be asked what shall we find? Ye will find the mercies of God to allure you, the influence of his holy spirit to guide you in right way to eternal life, Matt. vii, 8. *For every one that asketh receiveth*, but then my brethren we are to ask in a right manner, with faith and repentance, for except we repent we shall surely die, that is, we must suffer the wrath of the most high God, who will turn you away with this pronunciation *depart from me ye workers of iniquity*, Matt. vii, 23.[8] Therefore you see how dangerous a thing it is to live in any known sin, either of commission or omission, for if we commit any wilful [*sic*] sin, we become the servants of sin, John viii, 34. *Whosoever commiteth*

[sic] *sin is the servant of sin.* My dear brethren, have we not rendered ourselves too much the servants of sin, by a breach of God's holy commandments, by breaking his holy Sabbath, when we should have been sitting for our great and last change? Have we not been amusing ourselves with the pleasures of this life, or, if we have attended divine service, have we been sincere? For God will not be mocked, for he knows our thoughts. John iv, 24, *God is a spirit, and they that worship him must worship him in spirit and in truth.* Therefore my Brethren, we see how necessary it is that we should be sincere when we attempt to come to the Lord whether in public service or private devotion, for it is not the outward appearance but sincerity of the heart. This we must manifest by a holy life; for it is not every one that says Lord, Lord, shall enter into the kingdom of Heaven; but he that doth the will of my heavenly Father, Matt. vii, 21.

Therefore, we ought to come labouring and heavy laden to the throne of grace, and pray that God may be pleased to transform us anew in Christ Jesus. But it may be objected by those who have had the advantage of studying, every one is not calculated for the teaching of others. To those I answer, Sirs, I do not attempt to teach those who I know are able to teach me, but I shall endeavour by divine assistance to enlighten the minds of my brethren; for we are a poor despised nation, whom God in his wise providence has permitted to be brought from their native place to a christian land, and many thousands born in what are called christian families, and brought up to years of understanding. In answer to the objectors, Sirs, pray give me leave to enquire into the state of those children that are born in those christian families, have they been baptised, taught to read and learnt their catechism? Surely this is a duty incumbent on masters or heads of families.[9] Sirs, if you had a sick child, would you not send for a doctor?[10] If your house was on fire would you not strive to put it out to save your interest? Surely then you ought to use the means appointed to save the souls which God has committed to your charge, and not forget the words of Joshua, as for me and my house we will serve the Lord.[11] Children should be taught the fear of God: See what Solomon[12] says, Prov. viii, 18. *The fear of the Lord is to hate evil;*[13] chapter ix, 10. *The fear of the Lord is the beginning of wisdom;* chapter xiv, 17. *The fear of the Lord is a fountain of life.*[14] Here we see that children should fear the Lord.[15]

But I turn to my Brethren for whom this discourse is designed. My Brethren, if ye are desirous to be saved by the merits of Jesus Christ, ye must forsake all your sins, and come to the Lord by prayer and repentance of all your former sins, come labouring and heavy laden; for we are invited to come and rely on the blessed Jesus for eternal salvation. Matthew x, 32. *Whosoever shall confess me before men, him will I confess before my heavenly father.*[16] Here we have our Saviour's words of encouragement. See to it my brethren, that ye live a holy life, and that ye walk more circumspect or holy than ye have done heretofore. I now assure you that God is a spirit, and they that worship him must worship him in spirit and in truth; therefore if ye would come unto him, come as the poor publican[17] did, and say God be merciful to me a sinners; Luke xv, II. *And the publican standing afar off would not lift up so much as his eyes unto heaven, but smote upon his breast saying, God be merciful to me a sinner.*[18] For if we hope to be saved by the merits of Jesus Christ, we cast off all self-dependence, as to our own righteousness; for by grace ye are saved through faith, and that not of yourselves, it is the gift of God.

Here we see that the imperfections of human nature is such, that we cannot be saved by any other way but the name of Jesus Christ, and that there must be a principle of love and fear of God implanted in our hearts, if we desire to come to the divine fountain labouring and heavy laden with our sins. But the enquirer may enquire how do you prove this doctrine, are you not imposing on your brethren, as you know many of them cannot read. To this I answer, Sir, I do not mean to impose on my brethren, but to shew them there must be a principle of fear and love to God, and now I am to prove the doctrine that we ought to fear God, Psalm ciii, II.[19] *For as the heavens is high above the earth, so great is his mercy toward them that fear him. Verse* 13. *Like as a father pitieth his children, so the Lord pitieth them that fear him.* Psalm xxxiv, 9, *O fear the Lord ye his saints, for there is no want to them that fear him. Verse* II.[20] *Come ye children hearken unto me, I will teach you the fear of the Lord.* This may suffice to prove the doctrine that we ought to fear the Lord, here my brethren we see how much our salvation depends on our being transformed anew in Christ Jesus, for we are sinners by nature and are adding thereunto every day of our life, for man is prone to evil as the sparks to fly upward, this thought should put us on our guard against all manner of evil, especially of bad company.[21] This leads me to say, we should endeavour to glorify God in all our actions whether spiritual or temporal, for the apostle hath told us whatever we do, do all to the glory of God. 1 Cor. x. 30[22]

Let us now labour for that food which tendeth unto eternal life, this none can give but God only: My Brethren, it is your duty to strive to make your calling and election sure by a holy life, working out your salvation with fear and trembling, for we are invited to come without money and without price.

Isaiah lv I, *Ho every one that thirsteth come ye to the waters; and he that hath no money, come ye buy and eat; yea come and buy wine and milk without money and without price.* This leads me to say if we suffer as sinners, under the light of the gospel as sinners, the fault is in us, for our Saviour hath told us if he had not come we should not had sin, but now they have no cloak for their sins. Let us now improve our talents by coming labouring and burthened with a sense of our sins. This certainly is a necessary duty of all mankind, to come to the divine fountain for mercy and for the influence of God's holy spirit to guide us through this wilderness to the mansions of eternal glory.

My Brethren, have we not great encouragement to come unto the Lord Jesus Christ, Matthew vii. 7. *Ask and it shall be given you, knock and it shall be opened unto you.*[23] Therefore if ye desire to be saved by the merits of Christ, ye must come as the prodigal son did, Luke xv. 21. *And the son said unto him father I have sinned against Heaven and in thy sight, and am no more worthy to be called thy son.*[24] This is the language of the true penetent, for he is made sensible that there is no other name given by which he can be saved, but by the name of Jesus. Therefore we should put our trust in him and strive to make our calling election sure, by prayer and meditation. Psalm lv, I. *Give ear to my prayer O God, and hide not thyself from my supplication.*

But, my Brethren, are we not too apt to put off the thoughts of death till we are sick, or some misfortune happens to us, forgetting that bountiful hand who gives us every good gift: Doth not the tokens of morality call aloud to us all to prepare for death our great and last change, not flattering ourselves with the hopes of a long life, for we know not what a day may bring forth, therefore my Brethren let it be your greatest care to prepare for death, that great and irresistible [*sic*] king of terrors. Are we many of us advanced in years and we know not how soon God may be pleased to call us out of this life to an endless eternity, for this is the lot of all men, once to die, and after that the judgment. Let us now come to the Lord Jesus Christ, with a sense of our own impotency to do any good thing of ourselves, and with a thankful remembrance of the death of Christ who died to save lost man, and hath invited us to come to him labouring and heavy laden.[25] My ancient Brethren,[26] let us examine ourselves now whither we have had a saving change wrought in our hearts, and have repented of our sins, have we made it our greatest care to honor God's holy word and to keep his holy Sabbath's, and to obey his commandments.

Exodus xx. 6. *And shewing mercy to thousands of them that love me and keep my commandments,* have we been brought to bow to the divine sovereignty of the Most High God and to fly to the arms of the crucified Jesus, at whose crucifiction [*sic*] the mountains trembled, and the rocks rent, and the graves were opened and many bodies of saints that slept arose. Come my dear fellow servants and brothers, Africans by nation, we are all invited to come, Acts x. 34. *Then Peter opened his mouth and said, of a truth I perceive that God is no respecter of persons,* verse 35, *But in every nation he that feareth him is accepted of him.*[27] My Brethren, many of us are seeking a temporal freedom, and I wish you may obtain it; remember that all power in heaven and on earth belongs to God; if we are slaves it is by the permission of God, if we are free it must be by the power of the most high God. Stand still and see the salvation of God, cannot that same power that divided the waters from the waters for the children of Israel to pass through, make way for your freedom, and I pray that God would grant your desire, and that he may give you grace to seek that freedom which tendeth to eternal life, John viii, 32, *And ye shall know the truth and the truth shall make you free. Verse 36, If the Son shall make you free you shall be free indeed.*[28]

This we know my brethren, that all things work together for good to them that love God. Let us manifest this love to God by a holy life.

My dear Brethren, as it hath been reported that I had petitioned to the court of Hartford against freedom, I now solemnly declare that I never have said, nor done any thing, neither directly nor indirectly, to promote or to prevent freedom; but my answer hath always been I am a stranger here and I do not care to be concerned or to meddle with public affairs,[29] and by this declaration I hope my friends will be satisfied, and all prejudice removed. Let us all strive to be united together in love, and to become new creatures, for if any man be in Christ Jesus he is a new creature, 2 Cor. v. 17. *Therefore if any man be in Christ he is a new creature.* Old things are passed away behold all things are become new, now to be a new creature is to have our minds turned from darkness to light, from sin to holiness and to have a desire to serve God with our whole hearts, and to follow his precepts. Psalm xix, 10. *More to be desired than gold, yea than much fine gold, sweeter than honey and the honey comb.* Verse 11. *Moreover by them is they servant warned, and by keeping them there is great reward.*[30]

Let me now, my brethren, persuade you to prepare for death by prayer and meditation, that is the way, Matt. vi. *But when thou prayest enter into thy closet, and, when thou hast shut the door, pray to thy father in secret, and they father which seeth in secret shall reward thee openly.*[31]

My Brethren, while we continue in sin we are enemies to Christ, ruining ourselves, and a hurt to the commonwealth.[32]

Let us now, my brethren, come labouring and heavy laden with a sense of our sins, and let us pray that God may in his mercy be pleased to lift up the gates of our hearts, and open the doors of our souls, that the King of Glory may come in, and set these things home on our hearts. Psalm xxiv. 7. *Lift up your heads O ye gates, and be ye lifted up ye everlasting doors, amd* [sic] *the King of Glory shall come in*; then may we rely on the merits of Christ, and say, as David did, *In the Lord put I my trust*, Psalm ix. 4.[33] And again, *whom have I in heaven but thee, and there is none on earth I desire besides thee.*[34]

And now, my brethren, I shall endeavour to prove that we are not only ruining ourselves by sin, but many others. If the generality of men were more humble and more holy, we should not hear the little children in the street taking God's holy name in vain. Surely our conversation should be yea, yea, and nay, nay, or to that purpose. Matt. v. 7. *But let your communication be yea, yea, nay, nay, for whatsoever is more than these cometh of evil.*[35] Therefore my Brethren, we should endeavour to walk humble and holy, to avoid the appearance of evil; to live a life void of offence towards God and towards man. Hear what David saith, Psalm i, 1. *Blessed is the man that walketh not in the counsel of the ungodly nor standeth in the way of sinners.* Here we see how much it becomes us to live as christians, not in rioting and drunkenness, uncleanness, Sabbath breaking, swearing, taking God's holy name in vain; but our delight should be in the law of the Lord.[36]

The righteous man is compared to a tree that bringeth forth fruit in season. Psalm i, 3. *And he shall be like a tree planted by the rivers of water, that bringeth forth fruit in his season: His leaf also shall not wither, and whatsoever he doeth shall prosper.* Let us not forget the words of holy David, *man is but dust like the flower of the field.* Psalm ciii, 15.[37]

Let us remember the uncertainty of human life, and that we are many of us within a step of the grave, hanging only by the single thread of life, and we know not how soon God may send the cold hand of death and cut the thread of life: Then will our souls either ascend up to the eternal mansions of glory or descend down to eternal misery, our bodies lodged in the cold and silent grave, numbered with the dead, then shall the scripture be fulfilled, Gen. iii, 19. *In the sweat of thy face shalt thou eat bread, till thou return to the ground, for out of it wast thou taken, for dust thou art and unto dust thou shalt return.*

Now I am to call to the unconverted, my brethren, if we desire to become true converts we must be born again, we must have a spitual [sic] regeneration.[38] John iii, 3. *Verily, verily, I say unto you, except a man be born again he cannot see the kingdom of God.*

My brethren, are we not, many of us, ignorant of this spiritual regeneration? Have we seen our lost and undone condition without an interest in the merits of Jesus Christ; have we come weary and heavy laden with our sins, and to say with holy David, Psalm vi. 10. *Lord rebuke me not in thine anger, neither chasten me in thy hot displeasure.*[39] Hath it been our great care to prepare for death our great and last change, by prayer and meditation.

My dear brethren, though we are servants and have not so much time as we could wish for, yet we must improve the little time we have.

Mr. Burket,[40] a great divine of our church,[41] says, a man's hand may be on his plow and his heart in heaven, by putting up such prayers and ejaculations as these, Psalm lxi. I. *Hear my cry O God, attend to my prayer*, and again, *Whom have I in heaven but thee, and there is none on earth I desire besides thee.*[42]

We should pray that God would give us his holy spirit, that we may not be lead into temptation, and that we may be delivered from evil, especially the evil of sin. Rom. vi. 22, 23. *But now, being made free from sin, and become servants of God, ye have your fruit unto holiness, and the end everlasting life. For the wages of sin is death, but the gift of God is eternal life through Jesus Christ our Lord.*

My brethren, feeling I am desired by my friends to write something more than poetry, give me leave to speak plainly to you. Except you repent and forsake your sins ye must surely die.[43] Now we see how much it becomes us to break our alliance with sin and Satan, and to fly to a crucified Saviour, and to enlist under Christ's banner, and that he may give us grace to become his faithful subjects, should be our constant prayers. We should guard against every sin, especially against bad language.

Therefore, my Brethren, we should always be guarding against every evil word, for we are told that the tongue is an evil member, for with the tongue we bless God, and with the tongue we curse men. I Peter iii. 10. For he that loves life, and would see good days, let him refrain his tongue from evil and his lips from speaking guile.[44] But the thoughtless and unconverted sinner is going on in open rebellion, against that divine power which can in one minute cut the thread of life, and cast them away with this pronunciation, Depart from me ye workers of iniquity.[45] Matt. xxv. 41. *Then shall he say also unto them on the left hand, depart from me ye cursed into everlasting fire prepared for the devil and his angels.*[46]

And now, my brethren, shall we abuse the divine sovereignty of a holy God, who hath created us rational creatures, capable of serving him under the light of the Gospel, for he hath told us if he had not come unto us we had not had sin, but now we have no cloak for our sin.

Come now my dear brethren, accept of Jesus Christ on the terms of the gospel, which is by faith and repentance. Come labouring and heavy laden with your sins, and a sense of your unworthiness.

My Brethren, it is not we servants only that are unworthy, but all mankind by the fall of Adam, became guilty in the sight of God. Gen. ii. 17.[47] Surely then we are sinners by nature, and are daily adding thereto by evil practices, and it is only by the merits of Jesus Christ we can be saved, we are told that he is a Jew that is a Jew in his heart, so he is a Christian that is a Christian in his heart,[48] and it is not every one that says Lord, Lord, shall enter into the kingdom of God, but he that doth the will of God.[49] Let our superiors act as they shall think it best, we must resolve to walk in the steps our Saviour hath set before us, which was a holy life, a humble submission to the will of God. Luke xxii. 41, 42. *And he was withdrawn from them about a stones cast, and he kneeled down and prayed saying, father if thou be willing remove this cup from me, nevertheless not my will but thine be done.*[50]

Here we have the example of our Saviour who came down from heaven to save mankind, lost and undone without an interest in the merits of Jesus Christ, the blessed Jesus then gave his life a ransom for all that come unto him by faith and repentance; and shall not he that spared not his own son, but delivered him up for us all, with him freely give all things.

Come let us seek first, Christ, the kingdom of God; and his righteousness, all other things shall be added unto you. Matt. vi. 33.[51] Here we have great encouragement to come to the divine fountain.

Bishop Beverage[52] says, in his third resolution, the eyes of the Lord is intent upon us, he seeth our actions;[53] if our sins are not washed out with our tears, and crost with the blood of Christ, we cannot be saved. Come my brethren, O taste and see that the Lord is good, and blessed is the man that trusteth in him. Psalm xxxiv. 8.[54] Let us not stand as Felix did, and say, almost thou persuadest me to be a christian, but, let us strive to be altogether so.[55] If ye desire to become converts you must have a saving change wrought in your hearts that shall bring forth good works meet for repentance: Acts iii. 19. Repent ye therefore, be converted:[56] We are not to trust in our own strength but to trust in the Lord; Proverbs iii. 4. "Trust in the Lord with all thine heart, and lean not unto thine own understanding."[57]

My brethren, are we not incircled [*sic*] with many temptations, the flesh, the world and the devil; these must be resisted at all times. We must see to it that we do not grieve the holy spirit of God. Come let us my dear brethren, draw near to the Lord by faith and repentance for faith without works is dead. James ii. 20.[58] and Rom. x. 10. For with the heart man believeth, and with the mouth confession is made unto salvation.[59] Here we see there is something to be done by us as Christians; therefore we should walk worthy of our profession, not forgetting that there is a divine power which takes a just survey of all our actions, and will reward every one according to their works. Psalm lxii, 2. "Also unto the Lord belongeth mercy, for thou rememberest every man according to his works."[60] Therefore, it is our indispensable duty to improve all opportunities to serve God, who gave us his only son to save all that come unto him by faith and repentance.

Let me, my brethren, persuade you to a serious consideration of your danger while you continue in an unconverted state. Did you feel the operations of God's holy spirit, you then would leave all for an interest in the merits of Christ; "For the kingdom of heaven is like a treasure hid in a field; for which a man will sell all that he hath to purchase, Matt. x. 44.[61] So will every true penitent part with all for the sake of Christ. I shall not attempt to drive you to Christ by the terrors of the law, but I shall endeavor to allure you by the invitation of the gospel, to come labouring and heavy laden.

Matt. xi. 27.[62] Man at his best estate is like a shadow of the field. We should always be preparing for death, not having our hearts set on the things of this life: For what profit will it be to us, to gain the whole world and loose [*sic*] his own soul. Matt. xvi. 26.[63] We should be always preparing for the will of God, working out our salvation with fear and trembling. O may we abound in the works of the Lord. Let us not stand as fruitless trees or cumberers[64] of the ground, for by your works shall you be justified, and by your works shall you be condemned;[65] for every man shall be rewarded according to his works, Matt. xvi. 27. Let us then be pressing forward to the mark for the prize of the high calling of God in Christ Jesus. Let our hearts be fixed where true joys are to be found. Let us lay up treasures in Heaven, where neither moth nor rust doth corrupt, nor thieves break through nor steal. Matt. vi. 20.

Now I am come to contemplate the death of Christ, it remains I make a short contemplation. The death of Christ who died! Died to save lost man, I Cor. xv. 21. "For since by man came death, by man came also the resurrection from the dead: For as in Adam all died even so in Christ, shall all be made alive."[66] Let us turn to the scriptures, and there we shall see how our Saviour was denied by one and betrayed by another. Matt. xxvi. 14. Judas went unto the Chief Priest, and said, what will you give me, and they agreed for thirty pieces of silver, then they sought opportunity to betray him.[67] Verse 28. For this is my blood of the New Testament, which is shed for many for the remission of sins. Verse 33. Peter answered and said unto him, though all men should be offended because of thee, yet I will never be offended.[68] Verse 34. Jesus said unto him, verily I say unto thee, this night before the cock crow, thou shalt deny me thrice. Verse 38. Then said he unto them, my soul is exceeding sorrowful, even unto death: tarry ye here and watch with me. Verse 39. And he went a little further and fell on his face and prayed, saying, O Father, if it be possible, let this cup pass from me: Nevertheless, not as I will, but as thou wilt.[69]

My Brethren, here we see the love of God plainly set before us; that while we were yet sinners, he sent his son to die for all those that come unto him, labouring and heavy laden with a sense of their sins; let us come with a thankful remembrance of his death, whose blood was shed for us guilty worms out of the dust. Mat. xxvi. 63. But Jesus held his peace, and the High Priest answered and said unto him, I adjure thee by the Living God, that thou tell us, whether thou be the Christ the Son of God. And ver. 64 Jesus saith unto him, thou hast said: nevertheless I say unto you, hereafter shall ye see the Son of Man sitting on the right hand of power, and coming into the clouds of heaven. Verse 64.[70] Then the High Priest rent his clothes, saying, he hath spoken blasphemy; what further need have we of witness? Behold, now ye have heard his blasphemy. Here the High Priest charged the blessed Jesus with blasphemy: But we must believe that he is able to save all that come unto him, by faith and repentance. Matt. xxviii. 18. And Jesus came and spoke unto them, saying, all power is given unto me in heaven and on earth. As this should excite us to love and fear God, and to strive to keep his holy commandments, which is the only rule of life: But how apt are we to forget that God spoke these words, saying, I am the Lord thy God, which brought thee out of the land of Egypt and out of the house of bondage, Exod. xx. 1.[71] Thus we see how the children of Israel were delivered from the Egyptian service.[72]

But my brethren, we are invited to the blessed Jesus, who was betrayed by one and denied by another. Matt. xx. 24. The Son of Man goeth as it is written of him; but woe unto that man by whom the Son of Man is betrayed; it had been good for that man if he had never been born. Verse 24. Then Judas which betrayed him answered and said, Master is it I? He said unto him, thou hast said.[73]

Thus we see, my Brethren, that there is a woe pronounced agrinst [sic] every one that sins by omission or commission, are we not going on in our sins, and disobeying the word of God: "If ye love me, ye will keep my commandments."[74] Are we not denying the Lord Jesus, as Peter did. Matt. xxvi. 14.[75] Then began he to curse and swear, saying, I know not the man; and immediately the cock crew. And ver. 74.[76] And Peter remembered the words of Jesus, which he said unto him, before the cock crow thou shalt deny me thrice: And he went out and wept bitterly. Surely then we ought to come to the Divine Sovereign, the blessed Jesus who was crucified for us sinners. Oh! we ought to come on the bended knees of our souls, and say, Lord, we believe, help thou our unbelief.[77] Come my Brethren, let us cry to the life giving Jesus, and say, Son of God, have mercy on us![78] Lamb of God, that taketh away the sins of the world,[79] have mercy on us! Let us cast off all self-dependence, and rely on a crucified Savior. Luke. xxiii. 20. Pilate therefore, willing to release Jesus, spoke again to them. Verse 21. But they cried, saying, crucify him, crucify him. Here we may see the love of God, in giving his Son to save all that come unto him by faith and repentance. Let us trace the sufferings of our Saviour a little further: Matt. xxvi. 42. He went away again the second time, and prayed, saying, O my Father, if this cup may not pass away from me, except I drink it, thy will be done. Here we trace our Saviour's example set before us; so that we should not murmur at the hand of Divine Providence; for God hath a right to deal with his creatures as he pleaseth.

Come let us contemplate on the death of the blessed Jesus; and on the fearful judgment of the Lord passing on the guilty sinner. Luke xxiii. 30. Then shall they begin to say to the mountains, fall on us, and to the hills, cover us. Verse 32, 33. And there were also two malefactors led with him to be put to death; and when they were come to the place, which is called Calvary, there they crucified him and the malefactors, one on the right hand, and the other on the left; and thus was the scripture fulfilled. For he was numbered with transgressors. Matt. xxvii. 29. And when they had plated a crown of thorns, they put it upon his head, and a reed in his right hand. Verse 41, 42. Likewise the Chief Priest mocking him, with the Scribes and Elders, said, he saved others, himself he cannot save; If he be the king of Israel, let him come down from the cross, and we will believe him. Verse 44. Now from the sixth hour there was darkness over all the land unto the ninth hour.[80] Verse 46. And about the ninth hour Jesus cried with a loud voice, saying, Eli, Eli, Lama Sabachthani! This is to say, my God, my God, why hath thou forsaken me?

My brethern [*sic*],[81] should not a sense of these things on our mind implant in us a spirit of love to God, which hath provided a Saviour, who is able to save to the uttermost all that come unto him by faith and repentance, 2 Cor. vii. 10. For Godly sorrow worketh repentance to salvation, not to be repented of, but the sorrow of the world worketh death. My brethern [*sic*], see what sin hath done; it hath made all flesh guilty in the sight of God.

May we not adopt the language of David. Psal. lxxix. 8. O remember not against us former iniquities. Let thy tender mercies speedily prevent us. Psal. lxxx. 19. Turn us again, O Lord, God of Hosts, cause thy face to shine, and we shall be saved.

Let us contemplate a little further on the death of Christ. Matt. xxvii. 40.[82] Jesus, when he had cried with a loud voice, yeilded [*sic*] up the ghost. Ver. 4.[83] And behold the vail [*sic*] of the temple was rent in twain, from the top to the bottom; and the earth did quake, and the bricks rent. Here we see that the death of Christ caused all nature to tremble, and the power of heaven shaken: Here we may see not only the evil of sin, but also the unmeritted [*sic*] mercy of God, in giving his only Son. Should not our hearts be filled with fear and love to God; and we must believe that Jesus is the Son of God. Matt. xxvii. 54. Now when the Centurion and they that were with him, watching Jesus saw the earth quake, and those things that were done, they feared greatly, saying, truly, this was the Son of God. Now this was done for the remission of our sins, for without shedding of blood there is no remission of sin. This we have confirmed in the holy sacrament. Matt. xxvi. 27. For this is my blood of the New Testament, which was shed for many:[84] But the unbelieving Jews still persisted in their unbelief, and would have prevented the resurrection of our Saviour, if it had been in their power. Matt. xxvii. 62. The Chief Priests and Pharisees come together unto Pilate. Verse 63. Saying, Sir, we remember that the deceiver said, while he was yet alive, after three days I will rise again. Verse 66. So they went and made the sepulchre sure, sealing the stone and setting a watch.[85] Here we see the spirit of unbelief in Nathaniel. John i. 45 and 46. Philip findeth Nathaniel, and saith unto him, we have found him, of whom Moses in the law and the prophets did write, Jesus of Nazareth, the son of Joseph: And Nathaniel said unto him, can there be any good thing come out of Nazareth? Philip saith unto him, come and see. Thus we are to come and see the mercy of God, in sending his Son to save lost men. Let us contemplate on the manner of Christ's resurrection. Matt. xxv. 2. Behold there was a great earth-quake, for the angel of the Lord descended from heaven, and came and rolled the stone from the door and sat upon it.[86] Here we see that our Saviour was attended by an angel; one of those holy spirits we read of in the Revelations, vi. 8. They rest not day and night, saying, holy, holy, holy Lord God Almighty, which was and is, and is to come.[87] Ver. 4, 12. Saying with a loud voice, worthy is the Lamb, that was slain to receive power and riches, and wisdom and strength, and honor, and glory, and blessing.[88] And our Saviour himself tells us he hath received his power. Matt. xxviii. 19. And Jesus came and spoke unto them, saying, all power is given unto me in heaven and earth.[89] Then he gives his disciples their charge. Verse 19. Go ye, therefore, and teach all nations, baptizing them in the name of the Father, of the Son, and of the Holy Ghost. But I must conclude in a few words, and say,

My dear Brethren, should we not admire the free grace of God, that he is invit-ing of us to come and accept of Jesus Christ, on the terms of the gospel; and he is calling us to repent of all our sins: This we cannot do of ourselves, but we must be saved in the use of means not to neglect those two great articles of the Christian religion, baptism and the sacrament; and we ought all of us to seek by prayers: But the scripture hath told us, that we must not depend on the use of means alone. 1st Cor. iii. 6. The apostle says, I have planted Apolos[90] watered, but God gave the increase. Here we see if we are saved, it must be by the power of God's holy spirit. But my dear Brethren, the time is hastening when we must appear.

A POEM for Children with Thoughts on Death.

1. O YE young and thoughtless youth,   (*Eccle.* xii. I.
      Come seek the living God,
   The scriptures are a scared truth,
      Ye must believe the word.

2. Tis God alone can make you wise,   (*Prov.* iv. 7.
      His wisdom's from above,
   He fills the soul with sweet supplies
      By his redeeming love.

3. Remember youth the time is short,
      Improve the present day
   And pray that God may guide your thoughts,
      and teach your lips to pray.   *Psalm* xxx. 9.

4. To pray unto the most high God,
      and beg restraining grace,
   Then by the power of his word
      You'll see the Saviour's face.

5. Little children they may die,
      Turn to their native dust,
   Their souls shall leap beyond the skies,
      and live among the just

6. Like little worms they turn and crawl,
      and gasp for every breath,
   The blessed Jesus sends his call,
      and takes them to his rest.

7. Thus the youth are born to die,   *Psalm* ciii. 15.
     The time is hastening on,
  The Blessed Jesus rends the sky,
     and makes his power known.
8. Then ye shall hear the angels sing
     The trumpet give a sound,
  Glory, glory to our King,
     The Saviour's coming down.   *Matt.* xxvi. 64.
9. Start ye Saints from dusty beds,
     and hear a Saviour call,
  Twas Jesus Christ that died and bled,
     and thus preserv'd thy soul.
10. This the portion of the just,
     Who lov'd to serve the Lord,
  Their bodies starting from the dust,
     Shall rest upon their God.
11. They shall join that holy word,
     That angels constant sing,
  Glory glory to the Lord,
     Hallelujahs to our King.
12. Thus the Saviour will appear,   *Rev.* i. 7, 8.
     With guards of heavenly host,
  Those blessed Saints, shall then declare,
     Tis Father, Son and Holy Ghost.
13. Then shall ye hear the trumpet sound,
     The graves give up their dead,   *Matt.* xxvii, 51, 52.
  Those blessed saints shall quick awake,
     and leave their dusty beds.
14. Then shall you hear the trumpet sound,
     and rend the native sky,   I *Cor.* xv. 51, 52, 53, 54.
  Those bodies starting from the ground,
     In the twinkling of an eye.
15. There to sing the praise of God,
     and join the angelic train,
  And by the power of his word,
     Unite together again.

16. Where angels stand for to admit   *Matt.* iv. 8;[91]
        Their souls at the first word,
      Cast sceptres down at Jesus feet
        Crying holy holy Lord.
17. Now glory be unto our God
        all praise be justly given,
      Ye humble souls that love the Lord
        Come seek the joys of Heaven.
     HARTFORD, January 1, 1782

NOTES

1. This is the Roman numeral for the year 1782.

2. This quote is misattributed. The passage Hammon is quoting is actually from Matthew 10:32, "Whosoever therefore shall confess me before men, him will I confess also before my Father which is in heaven." Note that Hammon gets the verse number wrong, but also that there are some subtle changes to the wording of the verse in Hammon's paraphrase of the text. These types of misattributions and paraphrasing occur frequently in Hammon's works.

3. Hammon is referring here to the Samarian woman Jesus speaks to while visiting the Samarian city of Sychar just before he returns to Galilee for the first time since beginning his ministry. Samarians are an Israelite tribe that separated from Judaism after the Babylonian exile of 587–518 BCE. Samarians formed their own post-exilic societies, separate from mainstream Judaism, and were reviled by the Hebrew people of the time, which is why Jesus's followers were scandalized that he would speak with her at a well where they were drinking water and discussing the coming of the Messiah. The Samarian woman becomes a powerful symbol of faith within Christian tradition.

4. The actual quote for Psalms 31:1 is "In thee, O LORD, do I put my trust."

5. The quotation Hammon uses here is actually from Psalms 32:1, "Blessed *is he whose* transgression is forgiven, *whose* sin *is* covered." Notice, again, the subtle changes in the language of the paraphrase from the actual biblical quotation. The passage Hammon cites as the source of his quote, Psalms 33:7, actually states, "He gathereth the waters of the sea together as an heap: he layeth up the depth in storehouses."

6. Psalms 61:1 actually states, "Hear my cry, O God; attend unto my prayer." There is no single quote in the Bible that matches the paraphrase Hammon writes here. Hammon's wording seems to be an amalgam of several biblical passages. The construction, "*Have mercy on me, O God*," appears throughout the Bible but most closely matches part of Matthew 15:22, "Have mercy on me, O Lord, *thou* son of David." Hammon draws the construction, "*according to the loving kindness, according unto the multitude of thy tender mercies*," from Psalms 69:16, "Hear me, O Lord, for thy lovingkindness [*sic*] *is* good: turn unto me according to the multitude of thy tender mercies." And the construction, "*blot out my transgressions*," clearly comes from Psalms 51:9, "Hid thy face from my sins, and blot out all mine iniquities." All of these quotes do come from the Davidic Psalms, with the exception of the one from Matthew, which nevertheless is a quote of a Canaanite gentile woman recognizing

Jesus's lineage to David. The repeated reference to and identification of gentiles in the Bible seem to be an effort by Hammon to connect himself, as African descended, with being an outsider in the same sense as many gentiles who encounter Jesus. Hammon appears to be showing a unique ability to string together disparate biblical constructs to recreate passages that logically follow a *sense* of the meaning of the scriptures. He appears to be using similar literary techniques as do many of the writers of the Hebrew and Christian scriptures, borrowing from earlier writings to construct original verses that nevertheless are consistent with the literary and religious tradition. Perhaps this is an effort by Hammon to construct an original religious text suitable for him and his oppressed African-descended audience?

7. Matthew 5:8, "Blessed are the pure in heart: for they shall see God." Notice again the subtle change of wording. Hammon uses the word "poor," but in the King James Version it is "pure." What is at work here is a pattern of writing in which Hammon is emending to the Bible for his audience. I think Erskine Peters in his 1981 essay, "Jupiter Hammon: Engagement with Interpretation," attempts to begin looking into Hammon's interpretation and use of Christian doctrine to understand his social reality but does not go so far as to closely realize the depths to which Hammon appropriates and even changes the scriptures. Partly, Erskine focuses on Hammon poem, "Kind Master and Dutiful Servant," which is a paraphrase of several Christian ideas, but does not as fully engage with specific texts, like Hammon's longer essays or his poem to Phillis Wheatley.

8. Matthew 7:23, "And then I will profess unto them, I never knew you: depart from me, ye that work iniquity."

9. Hammon seems to be making an apology for slavery, suggesting that slavery is good because it has led to the Christianizing of African peoples in America. I suspect, however, that Hammon is actually using the circumstances of his social reality to engage in a type of moral suasion, to guilt masters of slaves to teach them to read and come to an understanding of the Bible and their catechisms independently. This is an interesting moment in Hammon's social thinking because he understands literacy to be a key to Christian salvation, a belief that will consequently lead to other types of social liberation.

10. This sentence is an oblique reference to Mark 2:17, Luke 5:31–32, and Matthew 9:12–13, all of which share a common source for the passage about sickness and salvation.

11. Joshua 24:15, "And if it seem evil unto you to serve the LORD, choose you this day whom you ye will serve; whether the gods which your fathers served that were on the other side of the flood, or the gods of the Amorites, in whose land ye dwell: but as for me and my house, we will serve the LORD." This is an interesting quotation for the fact that Joshua, in his old age, has just gathered together all of the tribes of Israel together to warn them not to return to worshipping the pre-flood gods of old or the gods of the nations surrounding them. Joshua is warning the Israelite *leaders* in this speech to do what is right in order to properly worship God. By comparison, Hammon is doing the same, but in an appeal to get the "masters" of the enslaved to baptize and *teach* their slaves to read as part of their duty to God. To do otherwise implies a backsliding into a sort of antediluvian state of transgression against God.

12. King Solomon was one of the greatest of the Hebrew kings. Many of the passages in the book of Proverbs are attributed to King Solomon, and Proverbs is one of the main biblical sources for Hammon's emphasis on fear as a motivator for proper conduct and faith.

13. The quote is actually from Proverbs 8:13.

14. The quote is actually from Proverbs 14:27.

15. Hammon is drawing his conclusions about the importance of fear from the "wisdom literature" of the Old Testament, a literature that "depicts a vital order informed by retributive justice and given human expression in wise utterance" (James G. Williams, *The Literary Guide to the Bible* 265). The motif of fear, particularly in children, is a problematic one, but makes some operative sense in the world-sense of American chattel slaves, whom Genovese noted in his work valued *order* as a valuable principle in a world of uncertainty and arbitrary decisions made by masters. Old Testament wisdom literature does not impose a systematic view of the world order and human behavior, rather, "individuals and situations are conceived of in their particularity and are not methodologically organized into a system of abstractions" (265–66). And though Hammon, himself, can be quite systematic in his *approach* to biblical exegesis/application, his reliance on wisdom literature to heavily influence his religious message is grounded in the practical wisdom of an easily accessible and concrete set of biblical pronouncements.

16. Compare this quotation from Matthew 10:32 with Hammon's earlier misquote from Matthew 10:33, "*Whosoever shall confess me before men, him will I confess before my heavenly father,*" which actually reads, "But whosoever shall deny me before men, him will I also deny before my Father which is in heaven." Hammon seems to conflate the two passages, Matthew 10:32 and Matthew 10:33. The two passages are in opposition to one another, establishing a warning, but Hammon seems to misquote Matthew 10:33 so that it is carries the same message, even wording, as 10:32.

17. A tax collector.

18. This passage is actually from Luke 18:13.

19. It appears that the typesetters for the essay used the Roman numeral for "II" instead of the number 11, which is appropriate for finding this quote (Psalms 103:11). I am able to detect many printers' interventions throughout Hammon's works. I suspect that many of these "interventions" may be due to the availability of type used to press the pages of Hammon's various writings. I try to account for these interventions throughout this edition.

20. This should read, Verse 11, but the printers use two consecutive letters "I."

21. Hammon's statement that, "for man is prone to evil as the sparks to fly upward . . ." is a direct reference to his belief in the Calvinist principle of total depravity, which is the concept that humanity has inherited a sinful nature due to the sin of disobedience committed by Adam and Eve in the garden of Eden. It follows from a long tradition of inherited corporate responsibility that stretches back to the ancient world. In Hammon's theology, depravity is only overcome by a true Christian conversion experience. See the first chapter of my book, *Evangelism and Resistance in the Black Atlantic, 1760–1835,* for a fuller explanation of the concept of depravity. Also see Jonathan Edwards's *The Works of Jonathan Edwards,* vol. 1, sect. 4.

22. "For if I by grace be a partaker, why am I evil spoken for that for which I give thanks? Whether therefore ye eat, or drink, or whatsoever ye do, do all to the glory of God" (1 Corinthians 10:30–31). Hammon paraphrases the second verse from this longer passage from Corinthians. The biblical passage, itself, is part of a larger set of instructions attributed to Paul explaining how a Christian ought to conduct him or herself as a guest to gentiles who might be pagan serving food that is against the laws of Judaism to eat. In this case, all food should be eaten unless it has been offered as a sacrifice to idols, in which case it is to be rejected. Hammon, however, is universalizing the passage to mean all activities one might conduct. Hammon clearly understands the specific application of the passage to food and eating, as illustrated by the following sentence in his essay; however, for Hammon, food and eating are merely metaphors for how one conducts himself or herself in life.

23. Hammon leaves out part of the verse, which reads, "Ask, and it shall be given you; seek, and ye shall find; knock, and it shall be opened unto you."

24. This is a paraphrase of Luke 15:21 in which the prodigal son returns to repent for wasting his inheritance. The parable of the prodigal son is ultimately a story of repentance and forgiveness that Jesus tells to the multitudes while on his way to Jerusalem, a biblical reference that fits well into this stage of Hammon's essay.

25. " . . . with a sense of our own impotency to do any good thing of ourselves . . ." Here Hammon alludes to the doctrine of "works righteousness," that Christian salvation cannot be accomplished as a result of any work or efforts a human being might put into achieving that state. Rather, it is only with salvation through faith that allows one to be saved and made of the elect. It is important to note, however, that faith is *not* the same as belief in the theology that Hammon subscribes to.

26. " . . . ancient Brethren . . ." Hammon is indicating that he is speaking specifically and directly to the African-descended peoples living in British North America, both enslaved and free. He also seems to be indicating that they are all descended from an ancient lineage, which could be indicative of him making a connection between the Black people in America and the Africans of the Bible.

27. The full verse states, "But in every nation he that feareth him, and worketh righteousness, is accepted with him."

28. Here Hammon purposefully conflates two different types of freedom, *temporal* and *spiritual*, as he also conflates the Old Testament understanding of Hebrew bondage in Egypt and the nation's subsequent temporal salvation with the New Testament version of freedom, which is wholly spiritual in nature. Hammon is folding several messages together here. The children of God have always sought temporal freedom, as illustrated in God's salvation of the Hebrew people from Egyptian bondage, a bondage God previously allowed as clearly indicated in the first chapter of Exodus. But Hammon also tries to impart the even more important message of *spiritual freedom*, as emphasized in the New Testament, that is also completely governed by God's will. The types of freedom, and the narratives that illustrate them, are explained in parallel in this brief passage.

29. " . . . I am a stranger . . ." This construction appears several times throughout the Bible ("I am a stranger and a sojourner," Genesis 23:4; "Why have I found grace in thine eyes, that thou shouldest take knowledge of me, seeing I am a stranger?" Ruth 2:10; "I am the son of a stranger," Samuel 1:13; "count me for a stranger: I am an alien in their sight," Job 19:15, etc.), and while Hammon may be alluding to one or more of those passages, it is more likely that he means this statement literally. Hammon was born and lived the majority of his life on Long Island, and he only spent occasional time in Hartford during the American Revolution when British forces occupied the Joseph Lloyd house and while on errands. As a literal stranger, it seems that Hammon was, at one point, accused of giving testimony against the idea of giving slaves their freedom after the war. He denies this charge but makes clear in a later essay that he is ambivalent about freedom for himself due to his advanced age and concern over his wellbeing as an elderly freedman with no caretaker. This paragraph is Hammon's defense of himself as a seeker for spiritual freedom over the temporal freedom since he sees one as more permanent than the other, but also recognizes the biblical precedent for temporal salvation as part of God's plan for Africans living in America.

It is also remotely possible that the "freedom" Hammon is referring to is the freedom from British rule near the end of the American Revolution. The date at the end of the poem that concludes the essay is January 1, 1782, which was the beginning of the year after several important American victories against the British. As the tide of the war had turned, it seemed inevitable by this time that the Americans were winning the war and serious discussions about the future destiny of the peoples living in the former colonies were being considered. The Lloyd family, whom he served, were ambivalent about taking sides in the war at first and had members of the family who fled America for England as dedicated loyalists. However, Hammon seems consistent in his poetry and prose as generally ambivalent to even expressing anti-war sentiments, such as in his 1783 poem "The Kind Master and the Dutiful Servant."

30. The passage actually says, "More to be desired *are they* than gold, yea, than much fine gold: sweeter also than honey and the honeycomb. Moreover by them is thy servant warned: *and* in keeping of them *there is* great reward" (Psalms 19:10–11).

31. Matthew 6:6, "But thou, when thou prayest, enter into thy closet, and when thou hast shut thy door, pray to thy Father which is in secret; and thy Father which seeth in secret shall reward thee openly."

32. Hammon is alluding to the idea that Great Britain is a *Christian Commonwealth*, so therefore sinfulness is counter to the principles and execution of the state.

33. Actually from Psalms 11:1.

34. Actually from Psalms 73:25.

35. Actually from Matthew 5:37.

36. This declaration of sins being committed in Hammon's eyes is not stated in a vacuum; rather, Hartford had been sacked and occupied by the British during the course of the war, which would have led to a tremendous amount of social disruption, but now, at the beginning of 1782, when the Americans are getting the upper hand against the British forces in the field, there may have been other types of social disruption associated with the war that Hammon is responding to.

37. Hammon is conflating verses 14 and 15 from Psalms 103. The two verses read, "For he knoweth our frame; he remembereth that we *are* dust. As for man, his days *are* grass: as a flower of the field, so he flourisheth." Hammon's conflation of the two sections of the text significantly changes the meaning. At first this conflated quote seems to allude to God's arbitrary power and the transience of human existence, but the Psalm, when read in its entirety, is a celebration of God's justice and mercy toward the oppressed. Though the Psalm reminds the reader of human transience, it also celebrates Gods mercy toward the oppressed humanity that fears Him and adheres to His commandments, "Like a father pitieth *his* children, so the Lord pitieth them that fear him" (Psalms 103:13). The entirety of this Psalm reads like the inspiration for the theme and imagery of Hammon's essay, focusing on God's sovereign power, righteousness, fear, children and childhood, and mercy toward the oppressed. This is particularly significant given the stated audience, his "Brethren," meaning enslaved and free African Americans.

38. "Regeneration" is the concept of shedding one's depravity through an actual, spiritually regenerative encounter with divinity. Christians at this time do not think of this as an intellectual or metaphorical encounter, but as a type of visitation brought on by one's faith.

39. This is actually from Psalms 6:1.

40. William Burkitt (1650–1703) was a Cambridge-educated English minister and vicar at Dedham, Essex. He is the author of several works of biblical exposition. Jupiter Hammon read at least one of Burkitt's books, *Expository Notes, with Practical Observations, on the New Testament* (published posthumously in 1724), which helped to inform some of the content of his essays "A Winter Piece" and an "Evening Improvement." See Leslie Stephen's *Dictionary of National Biography 7.*

41. " . . . our church . . ." This phrase is not meant to be a general reference to Christianity, but an indication of Hammon's identification with the Anglican faith. Many of the religious ideas he expresses are in accordance with Anglican orthodoxy, but later it will become apparent that some of his ideas depart from the mainstream of the church.

42. The second verse, "Whom have I in heaven but thee . . ." is from Psalms 73:25.

43. " . . . ye must surely die." This is an allusion to Genesis 2:17, "thou shalt surely die."

44. 1 Peter 3:10, " For he that will love life, and see good days, let him refrain his tongue from evil, and his lips that they speak no guile." At this stage in Hammon's essay, biblical quotations alternate between being italicized, being placed in quotation marks, or not being set apart from the rest of Hammon's own words by any markers at all. To this point in the text, biblical quotes and paraphrases were being italicized, but from this point forward, there is no consistency with how the printers mark biblical passages. I suspect that the printers were running out of italic type, so they resorted to ad-hoc methods for indicating (or not indicating) Hammon's quotes.

45. Psalms 6:8, "Depart from me, all ye workers of iniquity; for the LORD hath heard the voice of my weeping." This is another non-italicized biblical passage.

46. Hammon is linking these two biblical passages because of their use of the word "depart," and the seeming relationship with the casting away of those who bask in iniquity related to the use of "bad language," but the second passage is taken from a completely different context, following Matthew 25:40, "And the King shall answer and say unto them, Verily I say unto you, Inasmuch as ye have done *it* unto one of the least of these my brethren, ye have done *it* unto me." In this case, the transgression is not directly related to speech, such as cursing, but the transgression of not doing good for those in need.

47. This unmarked biblical reference reads, "But of the tree of the knowledge of good and evil, thou shalt not eat of it: for in the day that thou eatest thereof thou shalt surely die."

48. To clarify, Hammon is acknowledging that Jesus was a devout Jew, but that Jesus's followers hold their Christianity in their hearts in the same degree that Jesus held his Judaism in his own heart.

49. The last part of this sentence (" . . . and it is not every one who says Lord, Lord . . .") is a paraphrase of Matthew 7:21, "Not every one that saith unto me, Lord, Lord, shall enter into the kingdom of heaven; but he that doeth the will of my Father which is in heaven." This particular passage is taken from Jesus's warning against following false prophets.

50. Notice that the comparison here is not symmetrical. It is obvious that Hammon *is not* comparing his "superiors" with God in this paragraph, but he *is* comparing the enslaved and other black people of his time with Jesus, where he asks God to relive him of the burden of being crucified. Hammon is similarly asking his readers to use Jesus as an example, suggesting that they pray for salvation from bondage and prejudice but submit until such a time as God permits a change in the social order. It is important that when we read Hammon we notice the subtle yet ever-present appeals to a future without slavery. Hammon does not see his present moment in time as one of emancipation, but he *does* recognize and state, over and over, the spiritual equality of all humans, including masters and slaves. Couple this with the injunction to identify with Christ's example of carrying the burden of crucifixion, and we can see that Hammon is working out a *typology* connecting slavery with the labors of Christ.

51. The preceding sentence is another non-italicized biblical quote, Matthew 6:33, "But seek ye first the kingdom of God, and his righteousness; and all these things shall be added unto you." From this point on in the essay, biblical quotations are no longer italicized, and they are only sporadically indicated with quotation marks. This makes identifying the biblical passages more difficult for many

modern readers, given that Hammon's own language reads much like the English of the King James Bible, and also because the biblical quotations sometimes come before the chapter and verse markers and sometimes after. Readers should be aware of these shifts from this point on in the text.

52. William Beveridge (1637–1708), Bishop of Saint Asaph. Hammon had access to his book, *Private Thoughts Upon Religion, and a Christian Life.* See the *Dictionary of National Biography*, London: Smith, Elder & Co., 1885–1900.

53. Bishop Beveridge's third resolution from *Private Thoughts* states, "What is the reason why we ought to serve God so? Because *he searcheth the hearts, and understandeth all the imaginations of the thoughts*; that is, he is thoroughly acquainted with every thought in our hearts . . . and therefore hypocrisy is the most foolish and ridiculous sin imaginable, making as if we could cheat and deceive God, and hide our sins from the all-seeing eyes of Omniscience itself, of making God believe we are holy, because we appear to be so to men."

54. The sentence preceding the verse reference is the quote from Psalms Hammon indicates here.

55. This passage is an allusion to Acts 24:24–27.

56. The full passage of Acts 3:19 reads, "Repent ye therefore, and be converted, that your sins may be blotted out, when the times of refreshing shall come from the presence of the Lord." The Apostle Peter is speaking to the crowd of onlookers who have just watched Peter and John heal a lame man in the name of Jesus at the temple gate. Peter chastises the crowd for their participation in encouraging Pontius Pilot to crucify Jesus but also calls on them to repent and be forgiven and become followers of Jesus.

57. This quote is actually from Proverbs 3:5. Notice here how this biblical passage is set in quotation marks. I believe the printers of the essay have run out of italic type and are now improvising by setting biblical quotations apart with quotation marks or by not marking them apart from the surrounding text at all.

58. James 2:20, "But wilt thou know, O vain man, that faith without works is dead?" Here we come across a very stark contradiction between doctrines within Hammon's essay. On the one hand, he asserts that works are of no account toward the end of salvation, but here he quotes James's pronouncement that works are essential to the workings of faith. The Book of James, with his insistence on works as an important part of faith and salvation, has been a contentious text and doctrine within Protestant Christianity. In fact, Martin Luther, in his 1522 "Preface to the New Testament" ranked the Book of James as the least to the writings about Jesus and early Christianity, stating that the gospels and epistles of Saints John, Paul, and Peter "are the books that show Christ to you. . . . In comparison with these, the epistle of St. James is an epistle full of straw, because it contains nothing evangelical." See John Dillenberger, editor, *Martin Luther: Selections from His Writings* 19.

59. Romans 10:10, "For with the heart man believeth unto righteousness; and with the mouth confession is made unto salvation."

60. This is actually from Psalms 62:12.

61. There is no Matthew 10:44. The tenth chapter of Matthew only has forty-two verses. This quote is from Matthew 13:44 and reads, "Again, the kingdom of heaven is like unto treasure hid in a field; the which when a man hath found, he hideth, and for joy thereof goeth and selleth all that he hath, and buyeth that field."

62. It appears that the printers broke the paragraphs at the wrong spot. Matthew 11:27 refers to the final sentence of the previous paragraph, so should be where that paragraph ends. The sentence beginning "Man at his best estate . . ." should be the starting sentence of this current paragraph and

appears to be a conflation of Psalms 39:5, "Behold, thou hast made my days *as* an handbreadth; and mine age *is* as nothing before thee: verily every man at his best state *is* altogether vanity. Selah." And the passage from Psalms 144:4, "Man is like to vanity: his days *are* as a shadow that passeth away."

63. Readers will note that at this stage of the essay there is a shift in which some of the biblical quotes are coming *before* the citation and some *after*. For the rest of the essay, citations occur at random on either side of the quote they indicate.

64. One who cumbers, that is, to hamper, embarrass, hinder, get or be in the way of persons, their movements, etc.

65. Hammon has reworded the biblical passage from Matthew 12:37, which reads, "For by thy words thou shalt be justified, and by thy words thou shalt be condemned." He has exchanged the "words" with "works" in this passage, presumably to create a closer and more consistent parallel with the following passage from Matthew 16:27, which does state that believers will be rewarded "according to his *works*" [italics mine].

66. The passage actually reads, 1 Corinthians 15:21–22, "For since by man *came* death, also the resurrection of the dead. For as in Adam all die, even so in Christ shall all be made alive."

67. Hammon actually quotes Matthew 26:14–16, and it reads, "Then one of the twelve, called Judas Iscariot, went unto the chief priests, And said *unto them*, What will ye give me, and I will deliver him unto you? And they covenanted with him for thirty pieces of silver. And from that time he sought opportunity to betray him."

68. Matthew 26:33 actually reads, "Peter answered and said until him, Though all *men* shall be offended because of thee, *yet* will I never offend."

69. From this point forward in the essay, Hammon ceases to engage in exegesis and explanation and begins stringing together biblical passages to construct a unique narrative about the death of Jesus.

70. This should read, "verse 65." It is difficult to know whether the printer or Jupiter Hammon mistakenly cited the passage incorrectly.

71. Hammon is actually quoting Exodus 20:1–2, which reads in full, "And God spake all these words saying, I *am* the LORD thy God, which have brought thee out of the land of Egypt, out of the house of bondage." These first two verses of Exodus are God's preamble to the Ten Commandments as Moses spoke them to the masses at the base of Mount Sinai.

72. Notice Hammon's subtle use of language in this last sentence of the paragraph. He uses the word "service" rather than "slavery" or "bondage." He is making a very important point to his "Brethren," all of whom would have understood his message and his discreet use of language.

73. This entire paragraph is a quote from Matthew 26:24–25. This is another instance of a mistake in marking the proper chapter and/or verse that is hard to attribute to either Hammon or the printers.

74. This is from John 14:15.

75. This should read Matthew 26:74.

76. This should read "verse 75."

77. This phrase is taken from Mark 9:24, "And straightway the father of the child cried out, and said with tears, Lord, I believe; help thou mine unbelief." This is from the scene in the Book of Mark where Jesus casts out a demon from a child that had caused the boy frothing fits. His father, who was struggling to believe in miracles for the sake of his son, had brought the child to Jesus.

78. "…have mercy on us…" This construction occurs several times in relation to Jesus in Matthew and Luke. See Matthew 9:27, 20:30, 20:31, and Luke 17:13.

79. " . . . Lamb of God, which taketh away the sins of the world." This phrase occurs in John 1:29, when John the Baptist sees Jesus for the first time, "The next day John sees Jesus coming unto him, and saith, Behold the Lamb of God, which taketh away the sin of the world."

80. "Now from the sixth hour there was darkness . . ." This passage is actually from Matthew 26:45.

81. "Brethren" is misspelled only twice in the essay, and both instances are in this paragraph. It is difficult to know whether Hammon or the printers are responsible for this difference in the spelling.

82. This is actually in Matthew 27:50.

83. Actually this is Matthew 27:51.

84. This is actually a quote from Matthew 26:28, "For this is my blood of the new testament, which is shed for many for the remission of sins."

85. It is instructive to see the whole conversation between the priests, Pharisees, and Pilate, parts of which Hammon has edited out. Matthew 27:62–66 reads, "Now the Next day, that followed the day of preparation, the chief priests and Pharisees came together unto Pilate, Saying, Sir, we remember that the deceiver said, while he was yet alive, After three days I will rise again. Command therefore that the sepulchre be made sure until the third day, least his disciples come by night, and steal him away, and say unto the people, He is risen from the dead: so the last error shall be worse than the first. Pilate said unto them, Ye have a watch: go your way, make *it* as sure as ye can. So they went, and made the sepulchre sure, sealing the stone, and setting a watch."

86. This is actually Matthew 28:2.

87. This is actually from Revelation 4:8, which reads, "And the four beasts had each of them six wings about *him*; and they rest not day and night, saying, Holy, holy, holy, Lord God Almighty, which was, and is, and is to come." What the writer of Revelation depicts here, however, are not angels, but unidentified "beasts" with eyes in the front and back of their heads. The beasts also each had a different head, one like a lion, one like a calf, one like a man, and one like an eagle (See Revelation 4:6).

88. This is actually from Revelation 5:12.

89. This is actually from Matthew 28:18.

90. Apollos was a Christian Jew and a contemporary of Paul in the first century. He was born in Alexandria and is mentioned ten times in the New Testament as an eloquent teacher and defender of Christianity. Here, Hammon quotes the "apostle" Paul, noting that though Paul may have sent Apollos to teach and be a minister, it is God who actually does the spiritual work of conversion and bringing more people into the church.

91. This citation of Matthew 4:8 appears to be a mistake. Verse 16 of Hammon's poem is clearly a reference to Matthew 4:6, which is a dialogue between Jesus and the devil during the forty-day wilderness scene. However, the citation here points to the later passage where the devil tries to tempt Jesus with a promise to deliver him all of the kingdoms of the world to rule. This citation does not appear at all in the Stanley A. Ransom, Jr., edition of the poem.

A N
Evening's Improvement.
SHEWING,
The NECESSITY of beholding the LAMB of GOD.
To which is added,
A DIALOGUE,
ENTITLED,
The KIND MASTER and DUTIFUL SERVANT.

Written by JUPITER HAMMON, a Negro Man belonging to Mr. *John Lloyd*, of Queen's Village, on Long-Island, now in Hartford.

HARTFORD :
Printed for the Author, by the Assistance of his Friends

An Evening's Improvement, &c.

JOHN I. 29.
—*Behold the Lamb of God which taketh away the sins of the world.*

IN the begining [*sic*] of this chapter John bears testimony, that Jesus is the Son of God. Verse 1 st. In the beginning [*sic*] was the word, and the word was with God, and the word was God.[1] This is that Lamb of God which I now invite you to behold. My Brethren, we are to behold the Son of God as our Lord and giver of life; for he was made flesh and dwelt among us, verse 14[2] of the context, and here he is declared to be the Son of God full of grace and truth. And here in the first place I mean to shew the necessity of beholding the Lamb of God in the sense of the text. 2d. Endeavour to shew when we are said to behold the Son of God in the sense of the text. 3. I shall shew when we may be said not to behold the Lamb of God as we should do. In the 4th place I shall endeavor to shew how far we may be mistaken in beholding the Lamb of God. In the 5th place I shall endeavor to rectify these mistakes.³

My brethren, since I wrote my Winter Piece it hath been requested that I would write something more for the advantage of my friends, by my superiors, gentlemen, whose judgment I depend on, and by my friends in general, I have had an invitation to give a public exhortation; but did not think it my duty at that time; but now, my brethren, by divine assistance, I shall endeavor to shew the necessity of beholding the Lamb of God.⁴ My brethren we must behold the Lamb of God as taking away the sin of the world, as in our text, and it is necessary that we behold the Lamb of God as our King: ah! as the King immortal, eternal, invisible, as the only Son of God, for he hath declared him, as in the 8th verse of the context, no man hath seen God at any time: The only begotten Son, which is in the bosom of the Father, he hath declared him. My brethren, let us strive to behold the Lamb of God, with faith and repentance; to come weary and heavy laden with our sin, for they have made us unworthy of the mercy of the Lamb of God; therefore, we see how necessary it is that we behold the Lamb of God, in the sense of the text, that is, in a spritual [sic] manner, not having on our own righteousness; but we must be cloathed [sic] upon, with the unspotted robes of the Lamb of God; we must work out our salvation with fear and trembling, always abounding in the works of the Lord; we must remember the vows of our baptism, which is to follow the Lamb of God, John Chap. I. 33. Speaking of baptism, he saith, "upon whom thou shalt see the spirit descending and remaining on him, the same is he which baptiseth with the Holy Ghost," and verse 34, "and I saw, and bare record, that this is the Son of God," verse 35, "again the next day after, John stood and two of his disciples," verse 36, "and looking upon Jesus, as he walked, and saith, behold the Lamb of God," verse 37, and the two disciples heard him speak and they followed Jesus.⁵ Thus, my dear brethren, we are to follow the Lamb of God, at all times, whether in prosperity or adversity, knowing that all things work together for good, to them that love God, or as in Rom. viii. 28.⁶ now⁷ let us manifest that we love God, by a holy life; let us strive to glorify and magnify the name of the most high God. It is necessary that we behold the Lamb of God, by taking heed to our ways, that we sin not with our tongues, Psalm xxxix. 1.⁸ Here, my brethren, we have the exhortation of David, who beheld the Lamb of God with faith and love, for he crys [*sic*] out with a most humble petition, "O Lord, rebuke me not in thine anger; neither chastise me in thy hot displeasure." Psalm vi. 1. and now, my brethren, have we not great reason to cry to the Lamb of God, that taketh away the sin of the world, that he may have mercy on us and forgive us our sins, and that he would give us his holy spirit, that we may have such hungerings and thirsting as may be acceptable in the sight of God; for as the heart panteth for the water brook, so should our souls pant for the living God. Psalm xlii. 1.[9] and now, my brethren, we must behold the law of God, as is exprest [*sic*], John I. 51. "And he saith unto him, verily, verily I say unto you, hereafter you shall see heaven open, and the angels of God ascending and descending upon the Son of man." This is representation of the great day, when the Lamb of God shall appear. Matt. xxiv. 30, "and then shall appear the sign of the Son of Man in heaven, and then shall the tribes of the earth mourn, and they shall see the Son of Man coming in the clouds of heaven, with power and great glory." Here my brethren, we have life and death set before us, for if we mourn with the tribes for our sins, which have made us unworthy of the least favour in the sight of God, then he will have mercy and he will give us his holy spirit; then we shall have hearts to pray to the Lamb of God, as David did when he was made sensible of his imperfections, then he cryed [*sic*] to the Lamb of God, "have mercy upon me O God," Psal. lxi. 1, "according to thy loving kindness, according to the multitude of thy tender mercies, blot out my transgressions."[10] This my brethren is the language of the penitent, for he hath a desire that his heart may be turned from darkness to light, from sin to holiness;[11] this none can do but God; for the carnal mind is enmity against God, for it is not subject to the law of God, neither can be.[12] Here we see that we must behold the Lamb of God[13] as calling to us in the most tender and compassionate manner, Matt. xxiii. 37, saying, "O Jerusalem, Jerusalem, how often would I have gathered thy children together, even as a hen gathered her chickens under her wings, and ye would not."[14] As much as if he had said, O ye wicked and rebellious people have I not given my word as a rule of life; have I not sent the ministers of the gospel to teach you, and you will not receive the doctrine of the gospel, which is faith and repentance,[15] "I tell you nay; but except ye repent ye shall all likewise perish," Luke xiii. 4.[16]

And now my dear brethren, have we repented of our sins? Have we not neglected to attend divine service? Or if we have attended to the word of God, have we been sincere? For "God is a spirit, and they that worship him must worship him in spirit and truth," John iv. 24. When we have heard the word of God sounding in our ears, inviting of us to behold the Lamb of God; O my dear brethren, have we as it were laid up these words in our hearts, or have we not been like the stony ground hearers?[17] Matt. xii. 20. "But he that received the seed into stony places, the same is he that heareth the word, and anon with joy receiveth it." Verse 21. "Yet hath not root in himself, but dureth [*sic*] for a while; for when tribulation or perfection [*sic*] ariseth because of the word, by and by he is offended."[18] This is the effect of a hard heart. There is such a depravity in our natures that we are not willing to suffer any reproach that may be cast on us for the sake of our religion; this my brethren is because we have not the love of God shed abroad in our hearts; but our hearts are set too much on the pleasures of this life, forgetting that they are passing away; but the children of God are led by the spirit of God.[19] Rom. viii. 12, "Therefore brethren we are debtors, not to the flesh to live after the flesh." Verse 13, "For if ye live after the flesh ye shall die; but if through the spirit do mortify the deeds of the body, ye shall live." Verse 14, For as many are led by the spirit of God, they are the sons of God." Here my brethren we see that it is our indispensible [*sic*] duty to conform to the will of God in all things, not having our hearts set on the pleasures of this life; but we must prepare for death, our great and last change.[20] For we are sinners by nature, and are adding therunto by evil practices; for man is prone to evil as the sparks to fly upward;[21] and there is nothing short of the divine power of the most high God can turn our hearts to see the living and true God; and now we ought to behold the Lamb of God, as it is expressed in Isaiah vii. 14, "A virgin shall conceive and bear a son, and shall call his name Emanuel."[22] This my brethren is the Son of God, who died to save us guilty sinners, and it is only by the mercy of the blessed Jesus we can be saved: Therefore, let us call off self-dependence, and rely on a crucified Saviour, whose blood was shed for all that came unto him by faith and repentance; this we cannot do of ourselves, but we must be found in the use means; therefore we ought to come as David did, Psal. li. 1, "Have mercy on me O God, according to thy loving kindness."[23] This my brethren is the duty of all flesh to come to the divine fountain, and to confess our sins before the most high God; for "if we say we have no sin we deceive ourselves and the truth is not in us; but if we confess our sins he is faithful and just to forgive us our transgressions."[24] And now my brethren, seeing I have had an invitation to write something more to encourage my dear fellow servants and brethren, Africans, in the knowledge of the Christian religion, I must beg your patience, for I mean to use the utmost brevity that so important a subject will admit of; and now my brethren, we have as I observed in the foregoing part of this discourse, life and death set before us, for we are invited to come and accept of Christ on the terms of the gospel. Isaiah xliv. 1, "O every one that thirsteth, come ye to the waters, and he that hath no money, come ye buy and eat, yea, come ye buy wine and milk, without money and without price."[25] Here is life, and if we search our hearts, and try our ways, and turn again unto the Lord he will forgive us our sins and blot out our transgressions, Lamen, iii. 40.[26] But if we continue in our sins, having our hearts set on the pleasures of this life, forgetting that we must give an account for the deeds done in the body. Psal. lxii. 12, "Also, unto the Lord belongeth mercy, for he rendereth to every man according to his works."[27] Here we see that we should behold the Lamb of God by a holy life. Psal. vii. 11, "God judgeth the righteous and is angry with the wicked every day," verse 12, "if he turn not. He will whet his sword, he hath bent his bow and made it ready."[28] Here we see that the wrath of God abideth on the unbelievers and unconverted sinner.[29] And now my brethren, should not a sense of these things make us cry out in the apostle's language, 'Men and brethren what shall we do to be saved?'[30] We must be found in the use of means, and pray that God would be pleased to rain down a rain of righteousness into our souls; then we shall behold the Lamb of God as taking away the sins of the world.[31] Let us my brethren examine ourselves whether we have had a saving change wrought in our hearts, and have been brought to bow to the divine sovereignty of a crucified Saviour; have we been brought to behold the Lamb of God, by obeying the precepts of Isaiah, and turning from evil and learning to do well. Isaiah i. 16, "Wash ye, make you clean; put away the evil of your doing from before mine eyes; cease to do evil, learn to do well."[32] Here we have the admonition of the prophet Isaiah, who was inspired with the knowledge of divine things, so that he calls heaven and earth to witness against the wicked and rebellious sinner. Isaiah i. 2, "Here O heavens and give ear O earth; for the Lord hath spoken, I have nourished up children, and they have rebelled against me." Is not this the case? Have we not been going astray like lost sheep? Luke xv. 6,[33] Have we not great reason to lay our hands on our mouths and our mouths in the dust, and come upon the bended knees of our souls and beg for mercy as the publican did; saying, "God be merciful to me a sinner," Luke viii. 13.[34] This my dear brethren should be the language of our conversation; to have a life void of offence towards God and towards man. Have we beheld the Lamb of God, by taking up our cross, denying ourselves, and following the blessed Jesus. Matt. xvi. 24, "Then said Jesus unto his disciples, if any man will be my disciple, let him deny himself, take up his cross and follow me."[35] Here we see that we should behold the Lamb of God as our only Saviour and mighty Redeemer, and we are to take up our cross and follow the Lamb of God at all times, not to murmur at the hand of Divine Providence;[36] and we have our example set before us, Luke xxii. 41, 42, "And he was withdrawn from them about a stone's cast, and he kneeled down and prayed, saying, my Father, if thou be willing, remove this cup from me, nevertheless not my will but thine be done." We should behold the Lamb of God as coming in the clouds of heaven with great power and glory, whom our heavenly Father hath declared to be his only Son. Matt. xvii. 5, "And while he yet spoke, behold a bright cloud overshadowed them; and behold a voice out of the cloud which said, this is my beloved Son in whom I am well pleased, hear him." Should not a sense of these things inflame our hearts with fear and love to God; knowing that there is no other name given by which we can be saved, but by the name of Jesus; let us behold the Lamb of God as having power to make the blind to see, the dumb to speak, and the lame to walk, and even to raise the dead: But it may be objected and said by those that have had the advantage of studying, are we to expect miracles at this day? These things were done to confirm that Jesus was the Son of God, and to free us from the burthen of types and ceremonies of the Jewish law; and this by way of instruction, which I desire to receive with an humble spirit. Others may object and say, what can we expect from an unlearned Ethiopian? And this by way of reflection. To this I answer, Pray Sir, give me leave to ask this question, Doth not the raising of Lazarus give us a sight of our sinful natures? John xi. 12, 13, "And when he had thus spoken, he said with a loud voice, Lazarus come forth, bound hand and foot with grave clothes, and his head was bound with a napkin; Jesus saith unto them, loose him and let him go."[37] Is not this a simile of our deadness by nature? And there is nothing short of the power of the most high God can raise us to life. Sirs, I know we are not to expect miracles at this day; but hear the words of our Saviour Matt. xvi. 16, "And Simon Peter answered and said, thou art Christ the Son of the living God." Verse 17, "And Jesus answered and said unto him, blessed art thou Simon Barjona, for flesh and blood hath not revealed it unto thee, but my Father which is in heaven." Sirs, this may suffice to prove that it is by grace we are saved, and that not of ourselves, is the gift of God.[38] But my brethren, for whom this discourse is designed, I am now in the second place to shew when we are said to behold the Lamb of God in the sense of the text: When we are brought humbly to confess our sins, before the most high God, and are calling on our souls and all that is within us to bless his holy name; this is the duty of all flesh, to praise God for his unmerited mercy in giving his Son to save lost man, who by the fall of Adam became guilt in the sight of God. Rom. v. 8, "But God commandeth his love towards us, in that while we were sinners Christ died for us." Here we are to behold the Lamb of God as suffering for our sins, and it is only by the precious blood of Christ we can be saved, when we are made sensible of our own imperfections and are desirous to love and fear God; this we cannot do of ourselves, for this is the work of God's holy spirit. John vi. 64, "And he said, therefore said I unto you that no man can come unto me except it were given unto him, of my Father."[39] Here we see to behold the Lamb of God, in the sense of the text, as the gift of God; we should come as David did, saying, "O Lord rebuke me not in thine anger, neither chastise me in thy hot displeasure," Psal. vi. I. And we should put our whole trust in the Lord at all times; we should strive to live a religious life, to avoid the very appearance of evil,[40] least we incur the wrath of God. Psal. xi. 6, "Upon the wicked he shall rain showers of fire and brimstone and an horrible tempest; this shall be the portion of their cup."[41] Here we see the unhappy state of the sinner; for he is not only led away by that subtle adversary the devil, but he hath the word of God pronounced against him. Matt. xxv. 40, "Then shall he say unto them on the left hand depart from me ye cursed into everlasting fire prepared for the devil and his angels."[42] Here my brethren we are to behold the Lamb of God as being crucified for us Matt. xiii. 20,[43] Pilate therefore willing to release Jesus spake again to them. verse 22,[44] But they cryed [sic], saying crucify him, crucify him.[45] Here we see the effect of sin; the blood of Christ was shed for all that came unto him by faith and repentance. O my brethren, when those things have a proper influence on our minds, by the power of the most high God, to say as David did, Psal. ciii. I, "Bless the Lord O my soul, and forget not all his benefits."[46] Then we may be said to behold the Lamb of God in the sense of the text: And we are to behold the Lamb of God as it is expressed in Matt. xvii. 22, "And while they abode in Galille [sic] Jesus said unto them, the Son of Man shall be betrayed into the hands of men;" and verse 23, "And they shall kill him, and the third day he shall rise again." And now should not a sense of these things have a tendency to make us humble in the sight of God, and we should see the place and situation of Christ suffering. Luke xxii. 33, "And when they were come to the place called Calvary, there they crucified him, and the malefactors one on the right hand and the other on the left."[47] Here we see the boundless riches of free grace; he is numbered with transgressors, whole blood speaks better things than the blood of Abel; for the blood of Abel calls for justice on the sinner, but the blood of Christ calls for mercy. Luke xxiii. 34, "Then said Jesus, Father forgive them, for they know not what they do." Here we have the example of our Savior, that we should forgive our enemies, and pray that God would forgive them also, or how shall we say the Lord's Prayer, 'Forgive us our trespasses as we forgive them that trespass against us?'[48] Now when we are enabled to do these things, as we should do them, then may we be said to behold the Lamb of God in the sense of the text. And now my dear brethren, I am to remind you of a most melancholy scene of Providence; it hath pleased the most high God, in his wise providence, to permit a cruel and unnatural war to be commenced;[49] let us examine ourselves whether we have not been the cause of the heavy judgment; have we been truly thankful for mercies bestowed? And have we been humbled by afflictions? For neither mercies nor afflictions proceed from the dust, but they are the works of our heavenly Father; for it may be that when the tender mercies of God will not allure us, afflictions may drive us to the divine fountain. Let us now cast an eye back for a few years and consider how many hundreds of our nation and how many thousands of other nations have been sent out of time into a never-ending eternity, by the force of the cannon and by the point of the sword. Have we not great cause to think this is the just deserving of our sins; for this is the word of God. Isaiah iii. 11, "Wo [*sic*] unto the wicked, it shall be ill with him, for the rewards of his hands shall be given him." Here we see that we ought to pray, that God may hasten the time when the people shall beat their swords into ploughshares and their spears into pruning-hooks, and nations shall learn was no more.[50]

And now my dear brethren have we not great reason to be thankful that God in the time of his judgments hath remembered mercy, so that we have the preaching of the gospel and the use of our bibles, which is the greatest of all mercies; and if after all these advantages we continue in our sins, have we not the greatest reason to fear the judgments of God will be fulfilled on us. "He that being often reproved hardneth [*sic*] his neck shall suddenly be destroyed, and that without remedy."[51] Have we not great reason to praise God that he is giving us food and raiment, and to say as David did, Psal. cxxxvii. 1, "O give thanks unto the Lord, for his mercy endureth for ever."[52] And now my brethren, when these things make us more humble and more holy, then we may be said to behold the Lamb of God in the sense of the text. And now, in the third place, I am to shew when we may be said not to behold the Lamb of God in the sense of the text: When we are negligent to attend the word of God, and unnecessarily, or are living in any known sin, either of omission or commission, or when we have heard the word peached to us and have not improved that talent put into our hands by a holy life, then we may be said not to behold the Lamb of God in the sense of the text. And now my brethren, I am in the fourth place, to shew how in some things we may be mistaken in beholding the Lamb of God, while we are flattering ourselves with the hopes of salvations on the most slight foundation, because we live in a Christian land and attend to divine service; these things are good in themselves; but there must be a saving change wrought in our hearts, and we must become a new in Christ Jesus; we must not live after the flesh, but after the spirit, for as many as are led by the spirit of God are the sons of God, Rom. viii. 14.[53] and we are to pray that God would keep us from all evil, especially the evil of sin. Bishop Bevrage [*sic*], in his second Resolution, speaking of sin, he says, "For as God is the centre of all good, so sin is the fountain of all evil in that world, and strife and contention, ignominy and disgrace."[54] Read a little further, and goes on to protest against sin, "I resolve to hate sin (says he) wherever I find it, whether in myself or in others, in the best of my friends as well as in the worst of my enemies."[55] Here we see my brethren that if we commit any willful sin, either of omission or commission, we become the servants of sin, and are deceiving ourselves, for the apostle hath told us, that "the wages of sin is death," Rom. vi. 22, 23;[56] but now being made free from sin, and are become the servants of God ye have your fruits into holiness, and in the end eternal life; for the wages of sin is death, but the gift of God is eternal life through Jesus Christ our Lord. We are to behold the Lamb of God by reading the scriptures, and we must believe that he hath power to give everlasting life. John vi. 47, "Verily, verily I say unto you, he that believeth on me hath everlasting life." Do we my brethren believe in the blessed Jesus as we ought? Are we not going the broad way to utter destruction? Are we not leaving the blessed Jesus, who hath the bread of life and is that bread? John vi. 48, "I am the bread of life."[57] Here we see that the blessed Jesus hath power to give eternal life to all that come unto him by faith and repentance; and we see that he is calling to us as he did to his disciples, saying, "Wilt thou go away also;" for this is the language of the scriptures, John vi. 67, 68. "Then Simon answered him, Lord to whom shall we go? Thou hast the words of eternal life."[58] And we are my brethren to behold the Lamb of God as being the door of eternal life, for this he hath declared in his word to us. John x. 9, "I am the door, by me if any man enter he shall be saved, and shall go in and out and find pasture." But it is very plain my brethren that if we come in our sins God will not hears us, but if we come and worship him in spirit and in truth he will have mercy on us. John ix. 31, 32. "Now we know that God heareth not sinners, but if any man be a worshipper of God and doth his will, him he heareth." My dear brethren as I am drawing to a conclusion, let me press on you to prepare for death, that great and irresistible kings of terrors,[59] by a holy life, and make the word of God the rule of your life; but it may be objected we do not understand the word of God. Mr. Burkit [*sic*], a great divine of our church says, in the scriptures there is depths that an elephant may swim, and shoals that a lamb may wade.[60] Therefore we must take the plainest text as a key to us. And now my brethren I am in the fifth place to endeavor to rectify any mistake we may labour under, when we are taking on us the form of Godliness, without the power thereof, then we cannot be said to behold the Lamb of God in the sense of the text. We must pray earnestly to God for his holy Spirit to guide us in the way to eternal life; this none can do but God. Let us my brethren "lay up treasure in heaven, where neither moth doth corrupt nor thieves break through and steal." Matt. vi. 20—23,[61] Seek first the kingdom of God and his righteousness and all these things shall be added unto you. And now my dear brethren, we must pray earnestly to God for the influence of his holy spirit to guide us through this howling wilderness and sea of trouble to the mansions of glory, and we should pray that God would give us grace to love and to fear him, for if we love God, black as we be, and despised as we are, God will love us.[62] Acts x. 34. "Then Peter opened his mouth and said, of a truth I perceive that God has no respect to persons." Verse 35, "In every nation he that feareth him is accepted of him."[63] Psalm. xxxiv 8, "O taste and see that the Lord is good, and blessed is the man that trusteth in him." Verse 15, "The eyes of the Lord are upon the righteous, and his ears are open to their cry." Let us my dear brethren remember that the time is hastening when we shall appear before the Lamb of God to give an account for the deeds done in the body, when we shall be stumbling over the dark mountains of death looking into an endless eternity.[64] O that we may be of that happy number that shall stand with their lamps burning. Matt. xxv. 7, "Then all those virgins rose and trimmed their lamps."[65] Come now my brethren, let us examine ourselves whether we have had a saving change wrought in our hearts, and have been brought to bow to the divine sovereignty of the most high God, and to flee to the armies of Jesus, for he is the author of our peace, and the finisher of our faith. Heb. xii. 2, "Looking to Jesus the author and finisher of our faith."[66] Come now my brethren, we are one flesh and bone, let us serve the one living and true God.[67] Come let us behold the Lamb of God by an eye of faith, for without faith it is impossible to please God. Heb. xi. 5, For faith my brethren is of the things not seen.[68] Let us my brethren strive by the grace of God to become new creatures; for if any man be in Christ he is a new creature," 2. Cor. iv. 17.[69] Let us come to the divine fountain, by constant prayer. Psal. iv. 1, "Give ear to my words O Lord, consider my mediations," verse 2, 3.[70] Let us improve our talents by a holy life, striving to make our calling and election sure, for now is the accepted time; "behold now is the day of salvation." 2. Cor. vi. 2. Let us pray that God give us of the waters that the woman of Samaria drank. John xiv. 19, "But whosoever shall drink of the water I shall give him shall never thirst, but the water I shall give shall be in him a well of water springing up into everlasting life."[71] O my dear brethren we should be brought humbly to submit to the will of God at all times, and to say God be merciful to us sinners. Acts iii. 19, "Repent and be converted that your sins may be blotted out."[72] My dear brethren we are many of us seeking for a temporal freedom, and I pray that God would grant your desire; if we are slaves it is by the permission of God; if we are free it must be by the power of the most high God; be not discouraged, but cheerfully perform the duties of the day, sensible that the same power that created the heavens and the earth and causeth the greater light to rule the day and the lesser to rule the night, can cause a universal freedom; and I pray God may give you race to seek that freedom which tendeth to everlasting life. John viii. 32, "And ye shall know the truth, and the truth shall make you free." Verse 36, "If the Son shall make you free, then you shall be free indeed." But as I am advanced to the age of seventy-one years, I do not desire temporal freedom for myself.[73] My brethren, if we desire to be a happy people, we must be a holy people, and endeavor to keep the commandments of God, and we should pray that God would come and knock at the door of our hearts by the power of his holy spirit, and give us a steadfastness in the merits of Christ, and we are to believe in Christ for eternal salvation. Mr Stoddard, a great divine, says in speaking of appearing in the righteousness of Christ, when men believe it is part of God's covenant, to make them continue to believe.[74] Job vi. 12.[75] And again he saith, since God hath promised life unto all that believe in this righteousness, it must needs be safe to appear before God in this righteousness. Jer. iii. 22, "Return ye back-sliding children and I will heal your back-slidings; behold we come unto thee for thou art the Lord our God." My dear brethren let not your hearts be set too much on the pleasures of this life; for if it were possible for one man to gain a thousand freedoms, and had not an interest in the merits of Christ, where must all the advantage be; "for what would it profit a man if he should gain the whole world and loose his own soul," Matt. xvi. 26.[76] My brethren we know not how soon God may send the cold hand of death to summon us out of this life to a never-ending eternity, there to appear before the judgment seat of Christ. 2 Cor. v. 10, "For all must appear before the judgment seat of Christ."[77] And now I conclude with a few words—let me tell you my dear brethren, that in a few days we must all appear before the judgment seat of Christ, there to give an account for the deeds done in the body. Let us my brethren strive to be so prepared for death, by the grace of God, that when the time shall come when we are shaking off the shackles of this life, and are passing through the valley of the shadow of death. O may we then be enabled to say, come Lord Jesus come quickly, for thou art the Lamb of God, in whom my soul delighteth; Then my dear brethren all those which have repented of their sins shall hear this voice, "come unto me."[78] Matt. xxv. 34, "Then shall the King say unto them on his right hand; come ye blessed of my Father, inherit the kingdom prepared for you from the foundation of the world." But if we do not repent of our sins we must hear this voice, Matt. xxv. 41, "Then shall he say also unto them on his left hand, depart from me ye cursed into everlasting fire prepared for the devil and his angels." Then will our souls wast [sic] away into an endless eternity, and our bodies lodged in the cold and silent grave, there to remain till Christ's second coming. My brethren, we believe the word of God, we must believe this. I Cor. xxiii. 41, "Behold I shew you a mistery [sic], we shall not all sleep, but we shall be changed in a moment in the twinkling of an eye, at the last trumpet; for the trumpet shall sound and the dead shall be raised,"[79] verse 35,[80] "For this corruptible must put on incorruption and this mortals must put on immortality." And now my brethren, let me persuade you to seek the Lord. Isaiah lv. 6, "Seek the Lord while he may be found, and call on him while he is near;" verse 7, "Let the wicked forsake his way, and the unrighteous man his thoughts, and let him return unto the Lord, and he will have mercy on him, and to our God and he will abundantly pardon." Therefore not be contented with the form godliness without the power thereof.[81]   AMEN.

XXXXXXXX
XXXXXXX
XXXXXX
XXXXX
XXXX
XXX
XX
X

NOTES

1. See John 1:1.

2. John 1:14, which reads, "And the Word was made flesh, and dwelt among us, (and we beheld his glory, the glory as of the only begotten of the Father,) full of grace and truth."

3. Hammon names his text in these first six sentences and then proceeds to outline the order of his sermon, the order of his five arguments. This introductory statement is a standard convention of his period for the genre of sermon writing.

4. Hammon tells the reader here that his essay, "An Evening's Improvement," is the text of a sermon meant to be delivered to an audience. It is quite likely that Hammon meant "A Winter Piece" to be read out loud since he was clearly trying to reach an audience that would have included many who could not read.

5. A fuller context for this quote—without all of the breaks—clarifies what Hammon is trying to say regarding both baptism and the recognition of Jesus and salvation. John 1:32–37 states, "And John bare record, saying, I saw the Spirit descending from heaven like a dove, and it abode upon him. And I knew him not: but he that sent me to baptize with water, the same said unto me, Upon whom thou shalt see the Spirit descending, and remaining on him, the same is he which baptizeth with the Holy Ghost. And I saw, and bare record that this is the Son of God. Again the next day after John stood, and two of his disciples; And looking upon Jesus as he walked, he saith, Behold the Lamb of God! And the two disciples heard him speak, and they followed Jesus."

6. Romans 8:28, "And we know that all things work together for good to them that love God, to them who are the called according to *his* purpose."

7. Not capitalizing the beginnings of sentences is likely a result of the printing process the text underwent, but more analysis would be needed to determine the reason for this seeming lapse.

8. Psalm 39:1, "I said, I will take heed to my ways, that I sin not with my tongue: I will keep my mouth with a bridle, while the wicked is before me."

9. Hammon is paraphrasing Psalm 42:1 here, which reads, "As the heart panteth after the water brooks, so panteth my soul after thee, O God."

10. This quote is actually taken from Psalm 51:1. Hammon or the printers mistakenly attribute the quote to Psalm 61:1.

11. Hammon draws this paraphrase from Acts 26:18, "To open their eyes, *and* to turn *them* from darkness to light, and *from* the power of Satan unto God, that they may receive forgiveness of sins, and inheritance among them which are sanctified by the faith that is in me."

12. Here Hammon quotes Romans 8:7, "Because the carnal mind *is* enmity against God: for it is not subject to the law of God, neither indeed can be. Hammon does not mark the text as a quote but seems to assume his reader is familiar with the passage. These two verses from Acts 26:18 and Romans 8:7 are an instance of Hammon combining disparate biblical passages into a single message without identifying them as specifically biblical in origin.

13. It is notable that the construction, "behold the Lamb of God," which Hammon uses many times, is only written twice in the Bible, in John 1:29 and again soon after in John 1:36. These are the words of John the Baptist and are not seen anywhere else used in this combination.

14. The actual passage of Matthew 23:37 reads, "O Jerusalem, Jerusalem, *thou* that killest the prophets, and stonest them which are sent unto thee, how often would I have gathered thy children together, even as a hen gathereth her chickens under *her* wings, and ye would not!"

15. Notice here how Hammon boldly assumes the character and voice of Jesus, but these words are not written in the Bible; they are the work of Hammon, himself, taking artistic license to speak in the voice of Jesus.

16. "I tell you, Nay . . ." This quote actually comes from Luke 13:5.

17. Hammon is actually referencing Matthew 13:19. The phrase "stony ground hearers" refers to Matthew 13:20–22.

18. These two verses are misattributed and are actually from Matthew 13:20–22.

19. Once again, Hammon is emphasizing the significance of "depravity" as an inherent feature of being human. See note 42.

20. "Great and Last Change . . ." Though this is not a biblical phrase, it was popularly used in the eighteenth century and is usually read as an elaboration on Job 14:14, where Job contemplates the nature of death. I have been able to trace the origins of the phrase's use in America as far back as the late seventeenth century where it appears in the Reverend Ralph Wheelock's will of 1681. It appears to have been commonly used in wills as well as popular English publications, such as *The Gentleman's Magazine*, where the phrase occurs in the July 1785 edition on p. 505, books.google.com /books?id=PUsDAAAAMAAJ&pg=PA505&lpg=PA505&dq=%22great+and+last+change%22& source=bl&ots=y3Ptqen3rR&sig=KxTNJgEcJIoeGsNZio4vkgtF5RQ&hl=en&sa=X&ei=lX usU875ENOKqgaZnIHIAg&ved=0CBwQ6AEwADgK#v=onepage&q=%22great%20and%20 1ast%20change%22&f=false. It also appears on page 253 of *Mrs. Whittelsey's Magazine for Mothers and Daughters*, 1852, www.gutenberg.org/files/17775/17775-h/17775-h.htm. So while this phrase might sound biblical, it is actually a common phrase used to denote the coming of death or the end of life as a transformation or transition into a different state of spiritual being.

21. Hammon is paraphrasing Job 5:7, "Yet man is born unto trouble, as the sparks fly upward." Hammon uses this same phrase, "as the sparks fly upward," near the end of the ninth paragraph of "A Winter Piece."

22. In the Bible, the name is spelled "Immanuel." See Isaiah 7:14.

23. The full passage of Psalm 51:1 reads, "Have mercy upon me, O God, according to thy loving-kindness: according unto the multitude of thy tender mercies blot out my transgressions."

24. Hammon closely quotes John 1:8–9, which says, "If we say that we have no sin, we deceive ourselves, and the truth is not in us. If we confess our sins, he is faithful and just to forgive us *our* sins, and to cleanse us from all unrighteousness."

25. This quote is actually Isaiah 55:1 (not Isaiah 44:1) and states, "Ho, every one that thirsteth, come ye to the waters, and he that hath no money; come ye, buy, and eat; yea, come, buy wine and milk without money and without price."

26. Hammon is paraphrasing Lamentations 3:40, which actually reads, "Let us search and try our ways, and turn to the LORD."

27. Psalms 62:12 reads, "Also unto thee, O Lord, *belongeth* mercy: for thou renderest to every man according to his work."

28. Psalms 7:11–12, actually reads, "God judgeth the righteous, and God is angry *with the wicked* every day. If he turn not, he will whet his sword; he hath bent his bow, and made it ready." Hammon, as is characteristic of his writing, changes some of the wording in the verses, but it is not clear whether the punctuation is a result of his interventions or the printers'.

29. Here we see that Hammon is referencing John 3:36, which is the only place in the Bible that uses a similar construction of "the wrath of God abideth." John 3:36 reads, "He that believeth on the Son hath everlasting life: and he that believeth not the Son shall not see life, but the wrath of God abideth on him."

30. Acts 2:37, "Now when they heard *this*, they were pricked in their heart, and said unto Peter and to the rest of the apostles, Men *and* brethren, what shall we do?"

31. Hammon is paraphrasing 1 John 2:2, "and he is the propitiation of our sins: and not for ours only, but also for *the sins of* the whole world."

32. Here we see an interesting quote from the book of Isaiah, which is actually Isaiah 1:16 and part of the following verse 17, which reads, "Wash you, make you clean; put away the evil of your doings from before mine eyes; cease to do evil; Learn to do well; seek judgment, relieve the oppressed, judge the fatherless, plead for the widow."

33. Luke 15:6 reads, "And when he cometh home, he calleth together *his* friends and neighbours, saying unto them, Rejoice with me; for I have found my sheep which was lost."

34. Hammon or the printers mistakenly cite the wrong chapter of Luke. The quoted passage is in Luke 18:13, "And the publican, standing afar off, would not lift up so much as *his eyes* unto heaven, but smote upon his breast, saying, God be merciful to me a sinner."

35. Matthew 16:24 reads, "Then said Jesus unto his disciples, If any *man* will come after me, let him deny himself, and take up his cross, and follow me."

36. Hammon is making a reference to John 6:41–44, which says, "The Jews then murmured at him, because he said, I am the bread which come down from heaven. And they said, Is not this Jesus, the son of Joseph, whose father and mother we know? How is it then that he saith, I come down from heaven? Jesus therefore answered and said unto them, Murmur not among yourselves. No man can come to me, except the Father which hath sent me draw him: and I will raise him up at the last day."

37. Hammon or the printers cite the wrong verses. This quote is actually from John 11:43–44, which reads, "And when he thus had spoken, he cried with a loud voice, Lazarus, come forth. And he that was dead came forth, bound hand and foot with graveclothes: and his face was bound about with a napkin. Jesus said unto them, Loose him, and let his go."

38. This short section arguing the reality of biblical truths seems to be aimed at a different audience than the one Hammon identifies at the beginning of the sermon/essay. Instead of addressing slaves and free black people, Hammon appears to be addressing the ruling master class, who he realizes will also be reading his text.

39. This quote is actually from John 6:65.

40. 1 Thessalonians 5:22, "Abstain from all appearance of evil."

41. Psalms 11:6 actually reads, "Upon the wicked he shall rain snares, fire and brimstone, and a horrible tempest: *this shall be* the portion of their cup."

42. This quote is actually from Matthew 25:41.

43. This citation is a mistake. The part of the public trial leading up to the crucifixion Hammon is referencing here is actually located in Matthew 27:20–23.

44. Matthew 27:22.

45. This entire scene occurs in Matthew 27:20–23.

46. This is actually in Psalms 103:2.

47. This quote actually comes from Luke 23:33.

48. Hammon paraphrases the Lord's Prayer, which here is a conflation of passages from both Matthew 6:14–15 and Luke 11:4.

49. Hammon is referring to the American Revolutionary War (February 1775–September 1783). Hammon reveals in his writings a very negative attitude toward the war.

50. Hammon longs for the end of the Revolutionary War. He sees it as a senseless waste and shows in his writings that he saw that he had no stake in its outcome, either way.

51. Proverbs 29:1.

52. The quoted passage actually occurs in Psalms 107:1 and reads, "O give thanks unto the Lord for *he is* good: for his mercy *endureth* for ever."

53. Here Hammon is actually paraphrasing Romans 8:12–14, which reads, "Therefore, brethren, we are debtors, not to the flesh, to live after the flesh. For if ye live after the flesh, ye shall die: but if ye through the Spirit do mortify the deeds of the body, ye shall live. For as many as are led by the Spirit of God, they are the sons of God."

54. William Beveridge (1637–1708) was an episcopal minister and the Lord Bishop of St. Asaph in Denbighshire, north Wales. Hammon had access to his works in the Lloyd household and read *Private Thoughts Upon Religion, and A Christian Life, in Two Parts,* from which this quote is taken. In its entirety, the quote is actually the combination of two sentences from *Private Thoughts* and reads, "For, as God is the centre [*sic*] of all that is good, so is sin the fountain of all the evil in the world. All the strife and contention, ignominy and disgrace, misfortunes and afflictions, that I observe in the world; all the diseases of my body, and infirmities of my mind; all the errors of my understanding, and irregularities of my will and affections; in a word, all the evils whatsoever that I am effected with, or subject to, in this world, are still the fruits and effects of sin: for, if man had never offended the chiefest [*sic*] good, he had never been subject to this train of evils which attend his transgression" (*Private Thoughts* 112). This quote is pulled from the 1829 edition of the book; Hammon would have had an earlier edition of the Beveridge book.

55. See William Beveridge, *Private Thoughts* 112. Much of the direction in Hammon's thoughts on religion and biblical interpretation can be traced to the books on theology that he had access to, such as this one by Beveridge. It is important to recognize that Hammon's theology was not a simple, private one, but one informed by his reading beyond the Bible into the realm of theology and religious commentary.

56. The cited passage from Romans 6:22–23 reads, "But now being made free from sin, and become servants to God, ye have your fruit unto holiness, and the end everlasting life. For the wages of sin *is* death; but the gift of God *is* eternal life through Jesus Christ our Lord."

57. John 6:48 actually reads, "I am that bread of life."

58. John 6:67–68 reads, "Then said Jesus unto the twelve, Will ye also go away? Then Simon Peter answered him, Lord, to whom shall we go? Thou hast the words of eternal life." This is an important passage for Hammon since it speaks to the problem of belief. The passages just prior to John 6:67 relate how many of Jesus's followers in Capernaum left his ministry because his teachings had become too difficult to comprehend or even follow.

59. ". . . king of terrors . . ." This phrase is taken from Job 18:14, which reads, "His confidence shall be rooted out of his tabernacle, and it shall bring him to the king of terrors."

60. William Burkitt (1650–1703) was a vicar and biblical expositor whose *Expository Notes with Practical Observations on The New Testament* influences Hammon's writings and biblical thought. The particular passage that Hammon is citing here is from volume 2 of Burkitt's *Expository Notes* and reads, "That there are in the scripture truths suitable to the spiritual instruction and edification of all sorts of persons; there is in it both milk and strong meat, plain doctrines and first principles necessary for all, and truths of a deeper search that are profitable to some. 'In the scripture, said one, there are shallows and there are depths; fords where the lambs may wade, and depths where the elephants may swim.'" I could not determine who Burkitt appears to be quoting in the last sentence of this quotation.

61. Hammon paraphrases part of Matthew 6:20 and points the reader toward the rest of the passage, Matthew 6:20–23, which reads, "But lay up for yourselves treasures in heaven, where neither

moth nor rust doth corrupt, and where thieves do not break through nor steal: For where your treasure is, there will your heart be also. The light of the body is the eye: if therefore thine eye be single, thy whole body shall be full of light. But if thine eye be evil, thy whole body shall be full of darkness."

62. Here we see another rare but specific reference to the race and condition of Hammon's intended audience.

63. Acts 10:34–35 actually reads, "Then Peter opened *his* mouth, and said, Of a truth I perceive that God is no respecter of persons: But in every nation he that feareth him, and worketh his righteousness, is accepted with him." Hammon's choice of this passage is obvious for its reference to every "nation" having access to salvation, but it is also notable for the way it reduces the *status* of the believer to insignificance, so that in Hammon's world, slaves and their masters are equal in the eyes of divinity. This idea is repeated throughout Hammon's writings.

64. Hammon is making reference to Jeremiah 13:16, which reads, "Give glory to the LORD your God, before he causes darkness, and before your feet stumble upon the dark mountains, and, while ye look for light, he turns it into the shadow of death, *and* make *it* gross darkness."

65. This is in reference to the parable of the ten virgins that Jesus tells to his disciples on the Mount of Olives in Matthew 25:1–13.

66. The whole of Hebrews 12:2 reads, "Looking unto Jesus the author and finisher of *our* faith; who for the joy that was set before him endured the cross, despising the shame, and is set down at the right hand of the throne of God."

67. The construction "one flesh" appears throughout the Bible, but there is only one construction that contains "flesh" and "bone" such as we see here, and that is Judges 9:2, which reads, "Speak, I pray you, in the ears of all the men of Sachem, Whether *is* better for you, either that all the sons of Jerubbaal, *which are* threescore and ten persons, reign over you, or that one reign over you? Remember also that I *am* your bone and your flesh." In this passage Abimelech, Gideon's son by a Shechem concubine, is appealing to the men in his mother's city to support him in assassinating his brothers so that he may take control over part of Israel and become king of part of the nation. But it is difficult to see that Hammon wanted to make a literal connection between this passage and the point he is making in his essay. Rather, the sentence construction has a familiar aural pattern related to familial and national kinship that his audience would recognize and be able to relate intellectually and emotionally with the other familiar "one flesh" passages that relate to various forms of kinship.

68. Hammon is actually paraphrasing Hebrews 11:6–7 in both the previous sentences. The passages read, "But without faith *it is* impossible to please *him*: for he that cometh to God must believe that he is, and *that* he is a rewarder of them that diligently seek him. By faith Noah, being warned of God of things not seen as yet, moved with fear, prepared an ark to the saving of his house; by the which he condemned the world, and became heir of the righteousness which is by faith."

69. This quote actually occurs in 2 Corinthians 5:17, which reads, "Therefore if any man *be* in Christ, *he is* a new creature: old things are passed away; behold, all things are become new."

70. This quote actually comes from Psalm 5:1. Hammon does not quote or paraphrase verses 2 or 3, though he lists them here as relevant to his argument.

71. This quote is actually from John 4:14.

72. Acts 3:19 reads in its entirety, "Repent ye therefore, and be converted, that your sins may be blotted out, when the times of refreshing shall come from the presence of the Lord."

73. At the time Jupiter Hammon wrote this address, there were no laws in the state of New York to prevent owners of slaves from manumitting elderly slaves who had become unproductive laborers. In

many cases, elderly slaves who had been set free by their masters were rendered homeless and unable to make a living beyond begging. This became such a problem that the New York State Legislature enacted new laws in 1788—two years after Hammon's address was published in the state—to prevent slave owners from freeing slaves over the age of fifty without providing financial support as outlined by the new laws. See Thomas Greenleaf, *Laws of the State of New York, Comprising the Constitution and Acts of Legislature, Since the Revolution, From the First to the Fifteenth Sessions, Inclusive,* vol. 2, 1792.

74. Solomon Stoddard (1643–1729) was an influential American Congregationalist minister of Northampton, Massachusetts, and the grandfather of Jonathan Edwards. Hammon is making reference to Solomon Stoddard's book, *The Safety of Appearing at the Day of Judgment in the Righteousness of Christ, Opened and Applied* 114–15.

75. I am unable to discern why this passage is referenced here. Job 4:12 is a scene where Eliphaz, one of Job's comforters, is describing a dream he had about the relationship between guilt and suffering and does not seem to have anything to do with Hammon's arguments here.

76. Matthew 16:26 actually reads, "For what is a man profited, if he shall gain the whole world, and lose his own soul."

77. 2 Corinthians 5:10 actually reads, "For we must all appear before the judgment seat of Christ; that every one may receive the things *done* in his body, according to that he hath done, whether *it be* good or bad."

78. In the Bible, Jesus speaks these words many times, but Hammon's favorite passage that uses this phrase comes from Matthew 11:28, "Come unto me, all *ye* that labour and are heavy laden, and I will give you rest." This is a key text for Hammon's previous essay, "A Winter Piece."

79. This is actually from 1 Corinthians 15:51–52, which reads "Behold, I shew you a mystery; We shall not sleep, but we shall all be changed, In a moment, in the twinkling of an eye, at the last trump: for the trumpet shall sound, and the dead shall be raised incorruptible, and we shall be changed." Hammon or the printers attribute this passage to the wrong part of 1 Corinthians.

80. This should read "verse 53," pointing toward 1 Corinthians 15:53.

81. Hammon concluded his sermon with a paraphrase of 2 Timothy 2:4–5, which states, "Traitors, heady, highminded, lovers of pleasures more than lovers of God; Having a form of godliness, but denying the power thereof: from such turn away."

A DIALOGUE, *intitled,* *The* KIND MASTER *and the* DUTIFUL SERVANT, *as follows*: *Composed by* JUPITER HAMMON.

MASTER.

1. COME my servant, follow me,
   According to thy place;
   And surely God will be with thee,
   And send the heav'nly grace.

SERVANT.

2. Dear Master, I will follow thee,
   According to thy word,
   And pray that God may be with me,
   And save thee in the Lord.

MASTER.

3. My Servant, lovely is the Lord,
   And blest those servants be,
   That truly love his holy word,
   And thus will follow me.

SERVANT.

4. Dear Master, that's my whole delight,
   Thy pleasure for to do;
   As far as grace and truth's in sight,
   Thus far I'll surely go.

MASTER.

5. My Servant, grace proceeds from God,
   And truth should be with thee;
   Whence e'er you find it in his word,
   Thus far come follow me.

SERVANT,[1]

6. Dear Master, now without controul [*sic*],
   I quickly follow thee;
   And pray that God would bless thy soul,
   His heav'nly place to see.

MASTER.

7. My Servant, Heaven is high above,
   Yea, higher than the sky:
   I pray that God would grant his love,
   Come follow me thereby.

SERVANT.

8. Dear Master, now I'll follow thee,
   And trust upon the Lord;
   The only safety that I see,
   Is Jesus's holy word.

MASTER.

9. My Servant, follow Jesus now,
   Our great victorious King;
   Who governs all both high and low,
   And searches things within.

SERVANT.

10. Dear Master I will follow thee,
    When praying to our King;
    It is the Lamb I plainly see,
    Invites the sinner in.

MASTER.

11. My Servant, we are sinners all,
    But follow after grace;
    I pray that God would bless thy soul,
    And fill thy heart with grace.

SERVANT.

12. Dear Master I shall follow then,
    The voice of my great King;
    As standing on some distant land,
    Inviting sinners in.

MASTER.

13. My Servant we must all appear,
    And follow then our King;
    For sure he'll stand where sinners are,
    To take true converts in.

SERVANT.

14. Dear Master, now if Jesus calls,
    And sends his summons in;
    We'll follow saints and angels all,
    And come unto our King.

MASTER.

15. My Servant now come pray to God
    Consider well his call;
    Strive to obey his holy word,
    That Christ may love us all.

A LINE *on the present* WAR.

SERVANT.

16. Dear Master, now it is a time,
    A time of great distress;
    We'll follow after things divine,
    And pray for happiness.

MASTER.

17. Then will the happy day appear,
    That virtue shall increase;
    Lay up the sword and drop the spear,
    And nations seek for peace.

SERVANT.

18. Then shall we see the happy end,
    Tho' still in some distress;
    That distant foes shall act like friends,
    And leave their wickedness.

MASTER.

19. We pray that God would give us grace,
    And make us humble too;
    Let ev'ry nation seek for peace,
    And virtue make a show.

SERVANT.

20. Then we shall see the happy day,
    That virtue is in power;
    Each holy act shall have its sway,
    Extend from shore to shore.

MASTER.

21. This is the work of God's own hand,
    We see by precepts given;
    To relieve distress and save the land,
    Must be the pow'r of heav'n.

SERVANT.

22. Now glory be unto our God,
    Let ev'ry nation sing;
    Strive to obey his holy word,
    That Christ may take them in.

MASTER.

23. Where endless joys shall never cease,
    Blest Angels constant sing;
    The glory of their God increase,
    Hallelujahs to their King.

SERVANT.

24. Thus the Dialogue shall end,
    Strive to obey the word;
    When ev'ry nation act like friends,
    Shall be the sons of God.

25. Believe me now my Christian friends,
    Believe your friend call'd HAMMON:
    You cannot to your God attend,
    And serve the God of Mammon.

26. If God is pleased by his own hand
    To relieve distresses here;
    And grant a peace throughout the the land,[2]
    'Twill be a happy year.

27. 'Tis God alone can give us peace;
    It's not the pow'r of man:
    When virtuous pow'r shall increase,
    'Twill beautify the land.

28. Then shall we rejoice and sing
    By pow'r of virtues word,
    Come sweet Jesus, heav'nly King,
    Thou art the Son of God.

29. When virtue comes in bright array,
    Discovers ev'ry sin;
    We see the dangers of the day,
    And fly unto our King.

30. Now glory be unto our God,
    All praise be justly given;
    Let ev'ry soul obey his word,
    And seek the joys of Heav'n.

FINIS.

1. The printers appear to have inconsistently placed a comma here, at the end of the header for "Servant," instead of a period, like with all the other headers.

2. The double "the" in this line is in the original publication. I have chosen to retain it here as part of my effort to reveal the original readers' experience with Hammon's text, as well as show some of the peculiarities of eighteenth-century printing practices.

AN
ADDRESS
TO THE
NEGROES
In the STATE of NEW-YORK,[1]

By Jupiter Hammon,

Servant of JOHN LLOYD, jun, Esq; of the Manor of
Queen's Village, Long-Island

"Of a truth I perceive that God is no respecter of
"persons:
"But in every Nation, he that feareth him and
"worketh righteously, is accepted with him."—
Acts x. 34, 35.

NEW-YORK:
Printed by CARROLL and PATTERSON
No. 32, Maiden-Lane,
MDCC,LXXXVII.

To the Members of the AFRICAN SOCIETY,
in the city of NEW-YORK.

Gentlemen,
I Take the liberty to dedicate an address to my poor brethren to you. If you think
it is likely to do good among them, I do not doubt but you will take it under
your care. You have discovered so much kindness and good will to those you

thought were oppressed, and had no helper, that I am sure you will not despise what I have wrote, if you judge it will be of any service to them. I have nothing to add, but only to wish that "the blessing of many ready to perish, may come upon you."[2]

I am Gentlemen,
Your Servant,
JUPITER HAMMON.

Queen's Village, 24th Sept.
1786

To the PUBLIC.

As this Address is wrote in a better Stile [*sic*] than could be expected from a slave, some may be ready to doubt of the genuineness of the production. The Author, as he informs in the title page, is a servant of Mr. Lloyd, and has been remarkable for his fidelity and abstinence from those vices, which he warns his brethren against. The manuscript wrote in his own hand, is in our possession. We have made no material alterations in it, except in the spelling, which we found needed considerable correction.

The PRINTERS.
New-York, 20th. Feb. 1787.

AN
ADDRESS
TO THE
NEGROES
OF THE
STATE of NEW-YORK.

WHEN I am writing to you with a design to say something to you for your good, and with a view to promote your happiness, I can with truth and sincerity join with the apostle Paul, when speaking of his own nation the Jews, and say, "*That I have great heaviness and continual sorrow in my heart for my brethren, my kindsmen [sic] according to the flesh.*"[3] Yes, my dear brethren, when I think of you, which is very often, and of the poor, despised and miserable state you are in, as to the things of this world, and when I think of your ignorance and stupidity, and the great wickedness of the most of you, I am pained to the heart. It is at times, almost too much for human nature to bear, and I am obliged to turn my thoughts from the subject or endeavour to still my mind, by considering that it is permitted thus to be, by that God who governs all things, who seteth up one and pulleth down another.[4] While I have been thinking on this subject, I have frequently had great struggles in my own mind, and have been at a loss to know what to do. I have wanted exceedingly to say something to you, to call upon you with the tenderness of a father and friend, and to give you the last, and I may say dying advice, of an old man, who wishes your best good in this world, and in the world to come. But while I have had such desires, a sense of my own ignorance, and unfitness to teach others, has frequently discouraged me from attempting to say any thing to you; yet when I thought of your situation, I could not rest easy.

When I was at Hartford in Connecticut, where I lived during the war,[5] I published several pieces which were well received, not only by those of my own colour, but by a number of the white people, who thought they might do good among their servants. This is one consideration, among others, that emboldens me now to publish what I have written to you. Another is, I think you will be more likely to listen to what is said, when you know it comes from a negro, one your own nation and colour, and therefore can have no interest in deceiving you, or in saying any thing to you, but what he really thinks is your interest and duty to comply with. My age, I think, gives me some right to speak to you, and reason to expect you will hearken to my advice. I am now upwards of seventy years old,[6] and cannot expect, though I am well, and able to do almost any kind of business, to live much longer.[7] I have passed the common bounds set for man, and must soon go the way of all the earth. I have had more experience in the world than the most of you, and I have seen a great deal of the vanity, and wickedness of it. I have great reason to be thankful that my lot has been so much better than most slaves have had. I suppose I have had more advantages and privileges than most of you, who are slaves have ever known, and I believe more than many white people have enjoyed, for which I desire to bless God, and pray that he may bless those who have given them to me. I do not, my dear friends, say these things about myself to make you think that I am wiser or better than others; but that you might hearken, without prejudice, to what I have to say to you on the following particulars.

1st. Respecting obedience to masters. Now whether it is right, and lawful, in the sight of God, for them to make slave of us or not, I am certain that while we are slaves, it is our duty to obey our masters, in all their lawful commands, and mind them unless we are bid to do that which we know to be sin, or forbidden in God's word. The apostle Paul says, "Servants be obedient to them that are you masters according to the flesh, with fear and trembling in singlensess [*sic*] in your heart as unto christ: Not with eye service, as men pleasers, but as the servants of Christ doing the will of God from the heart: With good will doing service to the Lord, and not to me: Knowing that whatever thing a man doeth the same shall he receive of the Lord, whether he be bond or free."[8]—Here is a plain command of God for us to obey our masters. It may seem hard for us, if we think our masters wrong in holding us slaves, to obey in all things, but who of us dare dispute with God! He has commanded us to obey, and we ought to do it chearfully [*sic*], and freely. This should be done by us, not only because God commands, but because our own peace and comfort depend upon it. As we depend upon our masters, for what we eat and drink and wear, and for all our comfortable things in this world, we cannot be happy, unless we please them. This we cannot do without obeying them freely, without muttering or finding fault. If a servant strives to please his master and studies and takes pains to do it, I believe there are but few masters who would use such a servant cruelly. Good servants frequently make good masters. If your master is really hard, unreasonable and cruel, there is no way so likely for you to convince him of it, as always to obey his commands, and try to serve him, and take care of his interest, and try to promote it all in your power. If you are proud and stubborn an always finding fault, your master will think the fault lies wholly on your side, but if you are humble, and meek, and bear all things patiently, your master may think he is wrong, if he does not, his neighbours will be apt to see it, and will befriend you, and try to alter his conduct. If this does not do, you must cry to him, who has the hearts of all men in his hands, and turneth them as the rivers of waters are turned.[9]

2d: The particular I would mention, is honesty and faithfulness.

You must suffer me now to deal plainly with you, my dear brethren, for I do not mean to flatter, or omit speaking the truth, whether it is for you, or against you. How many of you are there who allow yourselves in stealing from your masters. It is very wicked for you not to take care of your masters goods, but how much worse is it to pilfer and steal from them, whenever you think you shall not be found out. This you must know is very wicked and provoking to God. There are none of you so ignorant, but that you must know that this is wrong. Though you may try to excuse yourselves, by saying that your masters are unjust to you, and though you may try to quiet your consciences in this way, yet if you are honest in owning the truth you must think it is as wicked, and on some accounts more wicked to steal from your masters, than from others.[10]

We cannot certainly, have any excuse either for taking any thing that belongs to our masters without their leave, or for being unfaithful in their business. It is our duty to be faithful, *not with eye service as men pleasers*. We have no right to stay when we are sent on errands, any longer than to do the business we were sent upon. All the time spent idly, is spent wickedly, and is unfaithfulness to our masters. In these thing I must say, that I think many of you are guilty. I know that many of you endeavour to excuse yourselves, and say that you have nothing you can call your own, and that you are under great temptations to be unfaithful and take from your masters.[11] But this will not do, God will certainly punish you for stealing and for being unfaithful. All that we have to mind is our own duty. If God has put us in bad circumstances, that is not our fault and he will not punish us for it. If any are wicked in keeping us so, we cannot help it, they must answer to God for it. Nothing will serve as an excuse to us for not doing our duty. The same God will judge both them and us.[12] Pray then my dear friends, fear to offend in this way, but be faithful to God, to your masters, and to your own souls.

The next thing I would mention, and warn you against, is profaneness.[13] This you know is forbidden by God. Christ tells us, "swear not at all,"[14] and again it is said "thou shalt not take the name of the Lord thy God in vain, for the Lord will not hold him guiltless, that taketh his name in vain."[15] Now though the great God has forbidden it, yet how dreadfully profane are many, and I don't know but I may say the most of you? How common is it to hear you take the terrible and awful name of the great God in vain?—To swear by it, and by Jesus Christ, his Son—How common is it to hear you wish damnation to your companions, and to your own souls—and to sport with in the name of Heaven and Hell, as if there were no such places for you to hope for, or to fear. Oh my friends, be warned to forsake this dreadful sin of profaneness. Pray my dear friends, believe and realize, that there is a God—that he is great and terrible beyond what you can think— that he keeps you in life every moment—and that he can send you to that awful Hell, that you laugh at, in an instant, and confine you there for ever, and that he will certainly do it, if you do not repent. You certainly do not believe, that there is a God, or that there is a Heaven or Hell, or you would never trifle with them. It would make you shudder, if you heard others do it, if you believe them as much, as you believe any thing you see with your bodily eyes.

I have heard some learned and good men say, that the heathen, and all that worshipped false Gods, never spoke lightly or irreverently of their Gods, they never took their names in vain, or jested with those things which they held sacred. Now why should the true God, who made all things, be treated worse in this respect, than those false Gods, that were made of wood and stone. I believe it is because Satan tempts men to do it. He tried to make them love their false Gods, and to speak well of them, but he wishes to have men think lightly of the true God, to take his holy name in vain, and to scoff at, and make a jest of all things that are really good. You may think that Satan has not power to do so much, and have so great influence on the minds of men: But the scripture says, *"he goeth about like a roaring Lion, seeking whom he may devour*[16]—*That he is the prince of the power of the air—and that he rules in the hearts of the children of disobedience,*[17]—*and that wicked men are led captive by him, to do his will."*[18] All those of you who are profane, are serving the Devil. You are doing what he tempts and desires you to do. If you could see him with your bodily eyes, would you like to make an agreement with him, to serve him, and do as he bid you. I believe most of you would be shocked at this, but you may be certain that all of you who allow yourselves in this sin, are as really serving him, and so just as good purpose, as if you met him, and promised to dishonor God, and serve him with all your might. Do you believe this? It is true whether you believe it or not. Some of you to excuse yourselves, may plead the example of others, and say that you hear a great many white-people, who know more, than such poor ignorant negroes, as you are, and some who are rich and great gentlemen, swear and talk profanely, and some of you may say this of your masters, and say no more than is true. But all this is not a sufficient excuse for you. You know that murder is wicked. If you saw your master kill a man, do you suppose this would be any excuse for you, if you should commit the same crime? You must know it would not; nor will your hearing him curse and swear, and take the name of God in vain, or any other man, be he ever so great or rich, excuse you. God is greater than all other beings, and him we are bound to obey. To him we must give an account for every *idle* word that we speak. He will bring us all, rich and poor, white and black, to his judgment seat. If we are found among those who *feared his name*, and *trembled at his word*, we shall be called good and faithful servants. Our slavery will be at an end, and though ever so mean, low, and despised in this world, we shall sit with God in his kingdom as Kings and Priests, and rejoice forever, and ever. Do not then, my dear friends, take God's holy name in vain, or speak profanely in any way. Let not the example of others lead you into the sin, but reverence and fear that great *and fearful name, the Lord our God.*[19]

I might now caution you against other sins to which you are exposed, but as I meant only to mention those you were exposed to, more than others, by your being slaves, I will conclude what I have to say to you, by advising you to become religious, and to make religion the great business of your lives.

Now I acknowledge that liberty is a great thing, and worth seeking for, if we can get it honestly, and by our good conduct, prevail on our masters to set us free: Though for my own part I do not wish to be free, yet I should be glad, if others, especially the young negroes were to be free, for many of us, who are grown up slaves, and have always had masters to take care of us, should hardly know how to take care of ourselves; and it may be more for our own comfort to remain as we are.[20] That liberty is a great thing we may know from our own feelings, and we may likewise judge so from the conduct of the white-people, in the late war.[21] How much money has been spent, and how many lives have been lost, to defend their liberty. I must say that I have hoped that God would open their eyes, when they were so much engaged for liberty, to think of the state of the poor blacks, and to pity us. He has done it in some measure, and has raised us up many friends, for which we have reason to be thankful, and to hope in his mercy. What may be done further, he only knows, for *known unto God are all his ways form the beginning.*[22] But this my dear brethren is by no means, the greatest thing we have to be concerned about. Getting our liberty in this world, is nothing to our having the liberty of the children of God. Now the Bible tells us that we are all by nature, sinners, that we are slaves to sin and Satan, and that unless we are converted, or born again, we must be miserable forever. Christ says, except a man be born again, he cannot see the kingdom of God, and all that do not see the kingdom of God, must be in the kingdom of darkness. There are but two places where all go after death, white and black, rich and poor; those places are Heaven and Hell. Heaven is a place made for those, who are born again, and who love God, and it is a place where they will be happy for ever. Hell is a place made for those who hate God, and are his enemies, and where they will be miserable to all eternity. Now you may think you are not enemies to God, and do not hate him: But if your heart has not been changed, and you have not become true christians, you certainly are enemies to God, and have been opposed to him ever since you were born. Many of you, I suppose, never think of this, and are almost as ignorant as the beasts that perish. Those of you who can read I must beg you to read the Bible, and whenever you can get time, study the Bible, and if you can get no other time, spare some of your time from sleep, and learn what the mind and will of god is.[23] But what shall I say to them who cannot read. This lay with great weight on my mind, when I thought of writing to my poor brethren, but I hope that those who can read will take pity on them and read what I have to say to them. In hopes of this I will beg of you to spare no pains in trying to learn to read. If you are once engaged you may learn. Let all the time you can get be spent in trying to learn to read. Get those who can read to learn you, but remember, that what you learn for, is to read the Bible. If there was no Bible, it would be no matter whether you could read or not. Reading other books would do you no good.[24] But the Bible is the word of God, and tells you what you must do to please God; it tells you how you may escape misery, and be happy for ever. If you see most people neglect the Bible, and many that can read never look into it, let it not harden you and make you think lightly of it, and that it is a book of no worth. All those who are really good, love the Bible, and meditate on it day and night. In the Bible God has told us every thing it is necessary we should know, in order to be happy here and hereafter. The Bible is a revelation of the mind and will of God to men. Therein we may learn, what God is. That he made all things by the power of his word; and that he made all things for his own glory, and not for our glory. That he is over all, and above all his creatures, and more above them that we can think or conceive—that they can do nothing without him—that he upholds them all, and will over-rule all things for his own glory. In the Bible likewise we are told what man is. That he was at first made holy, in the image of God, that he fell from the state of holiness, and became an enemy to God, and that since the fall, *all the imaginations of the thoughts of his heart, are evil and only evil, and that continually.*[25] *That the carnal mind is not subject to the law of God, neither indeed can be.*[26] And that all mankind, were under the wrath, and curse of God, and must have been for ever miserable, if they had been left to suffer what their sins deserved. It tells us that God, to save some of mankind, sent his Son into this world to die, in the room and stead of sinners, and that now God can save from eternal misery, all that believe in his Son, and take him for their saviour, and that all are called upon to repent, and believe in Jesus Christ. It tells us that those who do repent, and believe, and are friends to Christ, shall have many trials and sufferings in this world, but that they shall be happy forever, after death, and reign with Christ to all eternity. The Bible tells us that this world is a place of trial, and that there is no other time or place for us to alter, but in this life. If we are christians when we die, we shall awake to the resurrection of life; if not, we shall awake to the resurrection of damnation. It tells us, we must all live in Heaven or Hell, be happy or miserable, and that without end. The Bible does not tell us of but two places, for all to go to. There is no place for innocent folks, that are not christians. There is no place for ignorant folks, that did not know how to be christians. What I mean is, that there is no place besides Heaven and Hell. These two places, will receive all mankind, for Christ says, there are but two forts, *that is not with me is against me, and he that gathereth not with me, scattereth abroad.*[27]—The Bible likewise tells us that this world, and all things in it shall be burnt up—and that "God has appointed a day in which he will judge the world,[28] and that he will bring every secret thing whether it be good or bad into judgment[29]—that which is done in secret shall be declared on the house top."[30] I do not know, nor do I think any can tell, but that the day of judgment may last a thousand years. God could tell the state of all his creatures in a moment, but then every thing that every one has done, through his whole life is to be told, before the whole world of angels, and men. There, Oh how solemn is the thought! You, and I, must stand, and hear every thing we have thought or done, however secret, however wicked and vile, told before all the men and women that ever have been, or ever will be, and before all the angels, good and bad.

Now my dear friends seeing the Bible is the word of God, and every thing in it is true, and it reveals such awful and glorious things, what can be more important than that you should learn to read it; and when you have learned to read, that you should study it day and night. There are some things very encouraging in God's word for such ignorant creatures as we are; for God hath not chosen the rich of this world. Not many rich, not many noble are called, but God hath chosen the weak things of this world, and things which are not, to confound the things that are: And when the great and the rich refused coming to the gospel feast, the servant was told, to go into the highways, and hedges, and compel those poor creatures that he found there to come in.[31] Now my brethren it seems to me, that there are no people that ought to attend to the hope of happiness in another world so much as we do. Most of us are cut off from comfort and happiness here in this world, and can expect nothing from it. Now seeing this is the case, why should we not take care to be happy after death. Why should we spend our whole lives in sinning against God: And be miserable in this world, and in the world to come. If we do thus, we shall certainly be the greatest fools. We shall be slaves here, and slaves forever. We cannot plead so great temptations to neglect religion as others. Riches and honours which drown the greater part of mankind, who have the gospel, in perdition, can be little or no temptations to us.

We live so little time in this world that it is no matter how wretched and miserable we are, if it prepares us for heaven. What is forty, fifty, or sixty years, when compared to eternity. When thousands and millions of years have rolled away, this eternity will be no nigher coming to an end. Oh how glorious is an eternal life of happiness! And how dreadful, an eternity of misery. Those of us who have had religious masters, and have been taught to read the Bible, and have been brought by their example and teaching to a sense of divine things, how happy shall we be to meet them in heaven, where we shall join them in praising God forever. But if any of us have had such masters, and yet have lived and died wicked, how will it add to our misery to think of our folly. If any of us, who have wicked and profane masters should become religious, how will our estates be changed in another world. Oh my friends, let me intreat [sic] of you to think on these things, and to live as if you believed them to be true. If you become christians you will have reason to bless God forever, that you have been brought into a land where you have heard the gospel, though you have been slaves. If we should ever get to Heaven, we shall find nobody to reproach us for being black, or for being slaves. Let me beg of you my dear African brethren, to think very little of your bondage in this life, for your thinking of it will do you no good. If God designs to set us free, he will do it, in his own time, and way; but think of your bondage to sin and Satan, and do not rest, until you are delivered from it.

We cannot be happy if we are ever so free or ever so rich, while we are servants of sin, and slaves to Satan. We must be miserable here, and to all eternity.

I will conclude what I have to say with a few words to those negroes who have their liberty. The most of what I have said to those who are slaves may be of use to you, but you have more advantages, on some accounts, if you will improve your freedom, as you may do, than they. You have more time to read God's holy word, and to take care of the salvation of your souls. Let me beg of you to spend your time in this way, or it will be better for you, if you had always been slaves. If you think seriously of the matter, you must conclude, that if you do not use your freedom, to promote the salvation of your souls, it will not be of any lasting good to you. Besides all this, if you are idle, and take to bad couries [*sic*], you will hurt those of your brethren who are slaves, and do all in your power to prevent their being free. One great reason that is given by some for not freeing us, I understand is, that we should not know how to take care of ourselves, and should take to bad courses. That we should be lazy and idle, and get drunk and steal. Now all those of you, who follow any bad courses, and who do not take care to get an honest living by your labour and industry, are doing more to prevent our being free, than any body else. Let me beg of you then for the sake of your own good and happiness, in time, and for eternity, and for the sake of your poor brethren, who are still in bondage "*to lead quiet and peaceable lives in all Godliness and honesty,*"[32] and may God bless you, and bring you to his kingdom, for Christ's sake, Amen.

FINIS.

NOTES

1. I have edited this essay to include at its end a recently discovered poem written by Jupiter Hammon, which was composed at the same time as this "Address." It is my belief that the poem was intended by Hammon to be published at the end of his essay, in the same way that his other previous essays/sermons were followed by a poem written by him. In this way, it is my aim to present the text as Hammon originally intended for it to appear to the public.

2. This quote is actually a paraphrase of Job 29:13, "The blessings of him that was ready to perish came upon me: and I caused the widow's heart to sing for joy." In the biblical passage, Job is recalling his earlier adult life when he was a judge or public administrator, a time in which he is held in high esteem by those who come before him. See Walter A. Elwell, editor, *Baker Commentary on the Bible* 356–57. What Hammon appears to be indicating with this paraphrase is the esteem by which the New York African Society is held. It was a body dedicated to the relief of the suffering of African Americans in the city of New York, and thus petitioned for social justice.

3. This is a paraphrase of Romans 9:2–3, which reads, "That I have great heaviness and continual sorrow in my heart. For I could wish that myself were accursed from Christ for my brethren, my kinsmen according to the flesh."

4. Hammon expresses his predestinarian ideals about God and divine sovereignty here. The thinking expressed here was typical of many, if not most, followers of mainstream Anglicanism of the eighteenth century.

5. When British forces invaded Long Island, Hammon fled, along with his master, Joseph Lloyd, who was a Patriot. Hammon spent his time during the war between Hartford and New Haven.

6. Hammon was seventy-six years old on the publication of "An Address to the Negroes in the State of New-York."

7. Hammon's exact date of death is unknown, but it is documented that he was alive in 1792 (being listed in an inventory that year as property worth 16£), and he may have survived until 1805, which means he may have lived to as old as ninety-four. See "The Migration of Jupiter Hammon and His Family: From Slavery to Freedom and its Consequences," *Long Island History Journal*, vol. 23, no. 2. 2013, lihj.cc.stonybrook.edu/2013/articles/the-migration-of-jupiter-hammon-and-his-family-from-slavery-to-freedom-and-its-consequences/.

8. Here Hammon quotes Ephesians 6:5–8.

9. This sentence appears to be an allusion to Acts 1:24–25, which reads, "And they prayed, and said, Thou, Lord, which knowest the hearts of all *men*, shew whether of these two thou hast chosen, That he may take part of this ministry and apostleship, from which Judas by transgression fell, that he might go to his own place."

10. Hammon's views contrast with those of later former slaves when it comes to the matter of stealing from one's master. Contrast Hammon's attitude with that of Frederick Douglass's on the same subject in *My Bondage and My Freedom,* 1855.

11. Perhaps unwittingly, Hammon voices the legitimate claims of chattel slaves against their masters even while he chastises them. It is difficult to know the thinking of eighteenth-century slaves, as there were so few like Hammon, Wheatley, or Douglass who could read and write, but these paraphrases and indirect voicing of complaint might give insight into the mind and lived experiences of those multitudes of chattel slaves who could not communicate through their own written accounts.

12. Here we see Hammon struggling to reconcile slavery within a Christian context, and though the Bible through Paul, as he points out, clearly states that slaves should obey their masters, Hammon nevertheless consistently suggests that the institution of slavery and its practice may be sinful.

13. Specifically, Hammon means the use of profanity and bad language, though "profaneness" may also denote any unholy thought or activity.

14. Matthew 5:34.

15. Exodus 20:7.

16. 1 Peter 5:8, "Be sober, be vigilant; because your adversary the devil, as a roaring lion, walketh about, seeking whom he may devour."

17. Ephesians 2:2, "Wherein in time past ye walked according to the prince of the power of the air, the spirit that now worketh in the children of disobedience."

18. In the final phrase of this quote, Hammon seems to paraphrase several biblical versions of the construction, "wicked men are led captive" and "do his will" to construct the end of this passage.

19. Hammon quotes from Deuteronomy 28:58, "If thou wilt not observe to do all the words of this law that are written in this book, that thou mayest fear this glorious and fearful name, THE LORD THY GOD."

20. Here Hammon is referring to the unethical manumission of *elderly* slaves by their masters when those slaves have aged beyond their productive years. These elderly slaves would then be released into homelessness and begging in order to survive. This was a problem in New York, and it led to large numbers of homeless elderly, indigent former slaves. These slaves would die from hunger or exposure or would be exploited in the nominal welfare systems (operated by the Overseers of the

Poor) meant to help the impoverished, which were organized to exploit the labor of the poor instead and leave them with little to actually exist on.

21. Hammon is referring to the American Revolution.

22. Acts 15:18, "Known unto God are all his works from the beginning of the world."

23. It is important to emphasize here that Hammon is not just a "privileged" slave, but also one who was owned by Northeastern cosmopolitan masters who raised him to be literate and trusted him with errands and completing financial transactions. Literate slaves in New England would have been more common than on the southern and western plantations. Though Hammon surely saw brutality within the system, where he lived insulated him from some of the worst abuses that were committed within the system of chattel slavery, including the intense mistrust of the idea of literacy among slaves.

24. This is a bit disingenuous, for as I have shown earlier, Hammon has clearly read other books, mainly on theological matters, but nevertheless books other than the Bible in an attempt to understand his place in the world.

25. Genesis 6:5, "And God saw that the wickedness of man *was* great in the earth, and *that* every imagination of the thoughts of his heart *was* only evil continually."

26. Romans 8:7, "Because the carnal mind *is* enmity against God: for it is not subject to the law of God, neither indeed can be."

27. Matthew 12:30.

28. Acts 17:31.

29. Ecclesiastes 12:14, "For God shall bring every work into judgment, with every secret thing, whether *it be* good, or whether *it be* evil."

30. This is not a specific Bible passage, but a conflation of many sections mentioning secrets and revelations.

31. Luke 14:23, "And the lord said unto the servant, Go out into the highways and hedges, and compel *them* to come in, that my house may be filled."

32. This is a paraphrase of 1 Timothy 2:2, "For kings, and *for* all that are in authority; that we may lead a quiet and peaceable life in all godliness and honesty."

An Essay on Slavery, with submission to Divine providence, knowing that God Rules over all things— Written by Jupiter Hammon— [1]

1

Our forefathers came from Africa
tost over the raging main
to a Christian shore there for to stay[2]
and not return again.

2

Dark and dismal was the Day
When slavery began
All humble thoughts were put away
Then slaves were made *by Man.   *[to]

3

When God doth please for to permit
That slavery should be
It is our duty to submit
Till Christ shall [*make us free]   *[come again]

4

Come let us join with one consent
With humble hearts *and say   *[to]
For every sin we must repent
And walk in wisdoms way.

5
If we are free we'll pray to God
If we are slaves the same
*It's firmly fixt in [**his] word.   *[It is] **[his holy]³
Ye shall not pray in vain.

6
Come blessed Jesus in thy Love
And hear thy Children cry
And send them smiles now from above
And grant them Liberty.

7
Tis thou alone can make us free
We are thy subjects two⁴
Pray give us grace to bend a knee
The time we stay below.

8
This unto thee we look for all
Thou art our only King
Thou hast the power to save the soul
And bring us flocking in.

9
We come as sinners unto thee
We know thou hast the word
Come blessed Jesus make us free
And bring us to our God.

[10]⁵
Although we are in slavery⁶
We will pray unto our God
He hath mercy [~~hid~~] beyond the sky⁷
Tis in his holy word.

11
Come unto me ye humble souls
Although you live in strife
I keep alive, *I save the soul   *[and]
And give eternal life.[8]

12
To all that do repent of sin
[Be they] bond or free.[9]
I am their savior and their king
Hey must come unto me.

13
Hear the words *now of the Lord   *[of]
The call is loud and certain
We must be judged by his word
Without respect of person.

14
Come let us seek his precepts now
And love his holy word
With humble soul we'll surely[10] bow
And wait the *great reward.   [*undecipherable word rubbed out
                                        beneath "great"]

15
Although we came from africa
We look unto our God
To help with our hearts to sigh and pray
And love his holy word.

16
Although we are in slavery
Bound *by the yoke of Man   *[to]
We must always have a single Eye
And do the best we can.

17

Come let us join with humble voice
Now on the christian shore
If we will have our only choice
Tis Slavery no more.

18

Now [shurely]¹¹ let us not repine
And say his wheels are slow
He can fill our hearts with things divine
And give us freedom two.

19

He hath the power all in his hand
And all he doth is right
And if we are tide to [the] yoke of man
We'll pray with all our might.   [*We must pray through day and night.]¹²

20

This the State of thousands now
Who are on the christian shore
Forget the Lord to whom we bow
And think of him no more.

21

When shall we hear the joyfull sound
Echo the christian shore
Each humble [voice with songs resound]¹³
That Slavery is no more.

22

Then shall we rejoice and sing
Loud praises to our God
Come sweet Jesus heavenly king
Thou art the son [*Our Lord].   [*of God]

23

We are thy children blessed Lord
Tho still in Slavery
We'll seek thy precepts Love thy word
Untill the day we Die.

24

Come blessed Jesus hear us now
And teach our hearts[14] to pray
And seek the Lord to whom we Bow
Before tribunal day.

25

Now Glory be unto our God
All praise be justly given
Come seek his precepts Love his works
That is the way to Heaven.—
_____[15]

Composed By Jupiter Hammon
A Negro Man belonging to Mr John Lloyd
Queens-Village on Long Island—
November 10th 1786

Editor's Note: * The star indicates a word or passage that was changed by Jupiter Hammon as he corrected his manuscript. The word in brackets outside the line is the original word or phrase that was replaced by what appears clearly as the final version in this manuscript. There are several places in the original handwritten (holograph) manuscript where a word or phrase is rubbed out, leaving a faint impression, and then replaced. In most of these cases, the faint imprint left behind can still be read and allows us to know what Hammon's original wording was prior to correction.

NOTES

1. "An Essay on Slavery," a handwritten manuscript, was discovered in the Yale University Archives in 2011 among the Hillhouse Family Papers 282. It was not originally published with "An Address to the Negroes in the State of New-York"; however, it is my opinion that this was Jupiter Hammon's original intention since the poem was written at the same time as the "Address" with the

theme of slavery and freedom, a central topic of the "Address." It appears that the poem was left out of the original publication because of its unambiguous condemnation of slavery as a man-made sin rather than the will of God.

2. The word "Christian" is spelled with a lowercase "c" in all of Hammon's printed works, but the handwritten manuscript shows that Hammon alternated between an initial capital and lowercase letter "c."

3. The word "holy" is struck through on this line.

4. Hammon misspells the adverb "too" throughout the poem.

5. Here Hammon rubs out the stanza number and repositions it slightly to the right so that it aligns beneath stanza number "9." He seems to be very careful to make sure these stanza numbers line up on every page, as indicated by this correction.

6. In his holograph, Hammon switches between two different letter forms for the letter "s." I have not yet determined if there is a pattern for his use of one letter form over the other.

7. Hammon marks out the word "hid" on this line.

8. Here in stanza 11, Hammon switches voices from the narrative voice of the poet to that of God. He continues in the voice of God throughout stanzas 11 and 12, returning to the narrator's original voice again in stanza 13. The sudden shifting of voice is a technique that Hammon uses in other poems, particularly in "The Kind Master and the Dutiful Servant" and "An Address to Miss Phillis Wheatley."

9. Much of this line before "bond or free" is erased or struck out and replaced by the legible text "Be they."

10. The word "surely" is rubbed out here and then rewritten.

11. This word was rubbed out but is still legible. Hammon apparently did not intend for the word to be in the final version of the poem, but I add it here to help show Hammon's writing process.

12. This line was changed significantly from "We must pray through day and night" to its final form, "We'll pray with all our might."

13. The words after "Each humble" on this line were erased and rewritten, but the wording of both the original text and the corrections are difficult to discern. The phrase, "voice with songs resound" seems the most likely final correction, but the underlying, partially erased text appears to say, "[illegible] shall [illegible] around."

14. There is a rubbed-out word beneath "hearts" that is illegible.

15. The dashes that follow the last line of the poem were written as long wavy lines in the original holograph.

An Essay on Slavery, with submission to Divine
providence, knowing that God Rules over all things —
Written by Jupiter Hammon

1
Our forefathers came from Africa
tost over the raging main
to a Christian shore there for to stay
And not return again.

2
Dark and dismal was the Day
When Slavery began
All humble thoughts were put away
Then slaves were made by Man.

3
When God doth please for to permit
That slavery should be
It is our Duty to submit
Till Christ shall ~~make us free~~

4
Come let us join with one consent
With humble hearts ~~and~~ say
For every sin we must repent
And walk in wisdoms way.

5
If we are free we'll pray to God
If we are slaves the same
It's firmly fixt in his word
Ye shall not pray in vain.

6
Come blessed Jesus in thy Love
And hear thy Children cry
And send them smiles now from above
And Grant them Liberty.

7
Tis thou alone can make us free
We are thy subjects two
Pray give us grace to bend a knee
The time we stay below.

8
Tis unto thee we look for all
Thou art our only King
Thou hast the power to save the soul
And bring us flocking in.

On slavery 9 an Essay —

We come as sinners unto thee
We know thou hast the word
Come blessed Jesus make us free
And bring us to our God.

10

Although we are in slavery
We will pray unto our God
He hath mercy ~~and~~ beyond the sky
'Tis in his holy word.

11

Come unto me ye humble souls
Although you live in strife
I keep alive, and I save the soul
And give eternal Life.

12

To all that do repent of sin
~~Be they there~~ bond or free
I am their saviour and their king
They must come unto me.

13

Hear the words ~~anow~~ of the Lord
The call is loud and certain
We must be judged by his word
Without respect of person.

14

Come let us seek his precepts now
And love his holy word
With humble soul we'll ~~surely~~ bow
And wait the great reward.

15

Although we came from Africa
We look unto our God
To help our hearts to sigh and pray
And love his holy word.

16

Although we are in slavery
Bound by the yoke of Man
We must always have a single Eye
And do the best we can.

17

Come let us join with humble voice
Now on the christian shore
If we will have our only choice
'Tis slavery no more.

On slavery   an Essay —

18
Now ~~surely~~ let us not repine
And say ~~his~~ wheels are slow
Hee can fill our hearts with things divine
And give us freedom two.

19
Hee hath the power all in his hand
And all he doth is right
And if we are tide to the yoke of man
We'll ~~~ pray with all our might.

20
This the state of thousands now
Who are on the christian shore
Forget the Lord to whom we bow
And think of him no more.

21
When shall we hear the joyfull sound
Echo the christian shore
Each humble voice With songs resound
That slavery is no more.

22
Then shall we rejoice and sing
Loud praises to our God
Come sweet Jesus heavenly king
Thou art the son Our Lord

23
We are thy children blessed Lord
Tho still in slavery
Will seek thy precepts Love thy word
Untill the day we Die.

24
Come blessed Jesus hear us now
And teach our hearts to pray
And seek the Lord to whom we Bow
Before tribunal day.

25
Now Glory be unto our God
All praise be justly given
Come seek his precepts Love his works
That is the way to Heaven. —

Composed By Jupiter Hammon
A Negro Man belonging to Mr John Lloyd
Queens Village on Long Island — —

November 10th 1786

Bibliography

The Afro-American, "Notes on First Black Poet," April 18, 1970, no. 35, p. 3.

Beveridge, William. *Private Thoughts on Religion, and A Christian Life*. W. Collins & Co., 1827.

Bolton, Charla E., and Reginald H. Metcalf, Jr. "The Migration of Jupiter Hammon and His Family: From Slavery to Freedom and its Consequences." *Long Island History Journal*, vol. 23, no. 2, 2013, lihj.cc.stonybrook.edu/2013/articles/the-migration-of -jupiter-hammon-and-his-family-from-slavery-to-freedom-and-its-consequences/.

Brucia, Margaret A. "The African-American Poet, Jupiter Hammon: A Home-born Slave and his Classical Name." *International Journal of the Classical Tradition*, vol. 7, no. 4, 2001, pp. 515–22.

Burkitt, William. *Expository Notes with Practical Observations on the New Testament of Our Lord and Savior Jesus Christ, Wherein the Sacred Text is At Large Recited, The Sense Explained, and the Instructive Example of the Blessed Jesus, and His Holy Apostles, To Our Imitation Recommended*. Vol. II. Printed by J.R. and C. Childs, 1832.

Edwards, Jonathan. *The Works of Jonathan Edwards*. Vol 1, edited by Perry Miller. Yale UP, 1957.

Ferrers, Benjamin. *Dictionary of National Biography*. Smith, Elder & Co., 1885–1900.

Gates, Henry Louis, Jr., editor. *Norton Anthology of African American Literature*, 2nd ed. W.W. Norton & Co., 2004.

Genovese, Eugene D. *Roll, Jordan, Roll: The World the Slaves Made*. Vintage Books, 1976.

Greenleaf, Thomas, printer. *Laws of the State of New York, Comprising the Constitution and Acts of Legislature, Since the Revolution, From the First to the Fifteenth Sessions, Inclusive*. Vol. 2, 1792.

Hammon, Jupiter. "An Address to Miss Phillis Wheatley, Ethiopian Poetess, In Boston, who came from Africa at eight years of age, and soon became acquainted with the gospel of Jesus Christ," 1778.

———. "A Winter Piece: Being a Serious Exhortation, with a Call to the Unconverted: and a Short Contemplation on the Death of Jesus Christ," 1782.

———. "An Evening's Improvement. Shewing the Necessity of beholding the Lamb of God," to which is added, "The Kind Master and Dutiful Servant," 1783.

———. "An Essay on Slavery, With Justification to Divine Providence Knowing That God Rules Over All Things—Written by Jupiter Hammon." 1786. Yale University Library, Manuscripts and Archives, New Haven. Manuscript.

———. "An Address to The Negroes in The State of New-York." Printed by Carroll and Patterson, 1787.

"have, v." *The Oxford English Dictionary*, 2nd ed, 1989, Oxford UP, 30 April 2007, dictionary.oed.com/.

Hillhouse, Sarah Lloyd. Letter to Rebecca Woolsey. 19 July 1779. Hillhouse Family Papers. Yale University Library, Manuscripts and Archives, New Haven. Manuscript.

Johnson, Lonnell E. "Dilemma of the Dutiful Servant: The Poetry of Jupiter Hammon." *Language and Literature in the African American Imagination*, edited by Carol Aisha Blackshire-Berlay, Greenwood Press, 1992, pp. 105–17.

May, Cedrick. *Evangelism and Resistance in the Black Atlantic, 1765–1835*. The U of Georgia P, 2008.

May, Cedrick, and Julie McCown. "'An Essay on Slavery': An Unpublished Poem by Jupiter Hammon." *Early American Literature*, vol. 48, no. 2, 2013, pp. 457–71.

Nydam, Arlen. "Numeralogical Tradition in the Works of Jupiter Hammon." *African American Review*, vol. 40, no. 2, 2006, pp. 207–20.

Osann, Jean B. *Henry Lloyd's Salt Box Manor House*. Lloyd Harbor Historical Society, 1982.

Peters, Erkine. "Jupiter Hammon: His Engagement with Interpretation." *The Journal of Ethnic Studies*, vol. 8, no. 4, 1981, pp. 1–12.

Ransom, Stanley A. *America's First Negro Poet: The Complete Works of Jupiter Hammon of Long Island*. Kennikat Press, 1983.

Richards, Phillip M. "Nationalist Themes in the Preaching of Jupiter Hammon." *Literature*, vol. 25, no. 2, 1990, pp. 123–38.

Stephen, Leslie. *Dictionary of National Biography*. Vol. 7. British Library, Historical Print Editions, 2011.

Stoddard, Solomon. *The Safety of Appearing At the Day of Judgment, in the Righteousness of Christ, Opened and Applied*. Printed by Thomas M. Pomroy, 1804.

Townshend, Charles Hervey. *The British Invasion of New Haven, Connecticut: Together with Some Account of Their Landing and Burning The Towns of Fairfield and Norwalk, July 1779*. Printed by Tuttle, Morehouse & Taylor, 1879.

Wheatley, Phillis. "On Being Brought From Africa to America." *The Collected Works of Phillis Wheatley*. Edited by John Shields. Oxford UP, 1988, p. 18.

Index

Garth, George, xxiii-xxiv

handwritten, xii, xxxiv, xxxvi, 83n1, 84n2
Hillhouse, James, 15
history, xvi, xx, xxix, xxxiii
holograph, xiv-xv, xvii, 83, 84n6, 84n15
homeless, xxx-xxxi, 58n73, 77n20

intellectual, xi, xv, 36n38, 57n67
Interpretation, xiv-xv, xxiv, 33n7, 56n55

Johnson, Lonnell E., ix, xxvi, xxviii

king: Abimelech as, 57n67; Death as, 21,
    56n59; God as, 22–23; Jesus Christ as,
    1, 2, 28, 31, 37n46, 42, 52, 60–63, 80–82;
    King James Bible, xvi, 33n7, 38n51;
    Solomon as, 33n12
Koppell, Lillian, xv

labor, xxx, 37n50, 57n73, 78n20
liberation, xxiii, 33n9
liberty, xxix, xxxv, 65, 72–73, 75, 80
literacy, xi, 33n9, 78n23
literate, xxii, xxx, 78n23
Lloyd family, xi, xiv, xxi-xxii, xxxvi, 36n29;
    Harbor, xxii; Henry, xi, xxi, xxxviin3–4,
    1; household, xxi, xxii, xxvii, xxxvi, 56n54;
    James, xxxviin3; John, 17, 41, 65, 67, 83;
    Joseph, xxv-xxvi, 6, 12, 15, 35n29, 77n5;
    plantation, xi; Rebecca, xxi; Sarah, xxiv-
    xxvii, xxxviiin11
Loggins, Vernon, xii, xiv, xviin5, xxvii,
    xxxviin6
Lomax, Louis, xv, xxii
Long Island, xi-xii, xv, xviin1, xxi, xxv,
    xxxviin4, 35n29, 77n5,
Lord's Prayer, 48, 55n48
loyalty, xxi, xxvii, xxxiv, xxxviin3, 36n29

Mammon, 13, 63
manor house, xi, xxi
manumission, xxx, 57n73, 77n20
masculinity, xxix-xxx
Middle Passage, xxxi-xxxiv
Milton, John, ix, xxii, 2n1
monograph, xii-xiii
moon, xxi, xxiii
morality, xxxi, 21

New England, xi, xxxvi, 78n23
New-York Historical Society, xii, xv, xx,
    xxxvi
Nydam, Arlen, ix, xxviii

Obium, xi, xxi
occupation: of Hartford, x, 26n36; of Long
    Island, xxv, 35n29
O'Neale, Sondra A., ix, xii, xxviii
Overseers of the poor, 77n20

pagan, xxxii, 34n22
patriot, xxiv, 77n5
Paul of Tarsus, xxvi, xxxiv, 34n22, 38n58,
    40n90, 68–69, 77n12
political, xi, xv, xxvii, xxix
Pope, Alexander, xxii-xxiii
prayer, act of, ix, 2, 18, 19, 21, 22, 24, 30, 32,
    50
Puritan, ix

Ransom, Stanley A., Jr., xii-xiv, xviin5–6,
    xxvii, xxxviin6, 40n91
research, xii-xiii, xiv-xv, xxiii, xxviii
researchers, xii, xvi, xxxvi
resistance, xiii, xxix, xxx,
Revolutionary War, x, xi, xxiv, 55n49–50
Richards, Phillip M., ix, xxviii
Rose, xi, xxi,

scholarship, xiii—xv, xxvi, xxviii, xxix

sickness, xxxv, 3, 19, 21, 33n10

spiritual, xv, 20, 37n50, 56n60; freedom, x, xxvi, 35n28–29; salvation, xxiii, 23, 36n38, 40n90, 54n20; wealth, ix, 13n1

Sterling Memorial Library (Yale), xii, xx, xxv

Stiles, Ezra, xxiv, xxxviiin9

Stoddard, Solomon, 51, 58n74

stranger, xxvi, 22, 35n29

suicide, xxvi

sun, 2n4,

temporal, xxiii–xxvii, xxix, 20, 22, 35n28–29, 51

theological, xiv, xv, xxxiii–xxxiv, 78n24

theology, xxxiv, 34n21, 35n25, 56n55

Townsend, Phebe, xxxvi, 6

transcription, xvii, xxxvi

twentieth century, xii, xv, xxii, xxxviin6

Tyron, William, xxii

Verantes, Charles A., xv

verna, xxi

virtue, xxv, 61–63

Washington, George, xxiii

Wegelin, Oscar, xii, xiii, xv, xviin4, xxxviin6

Wheatley, Phillis, ix; relating to "An Address," xxxi–xxxiii, xxxv–xxxvi, 11–12, 33, 84; slavery, 77n11

Yale University, xii, xx, xxiv, xxv, xxvii, xxxviiin9, xxxviiin11 l